The Treasury of Christ

A Commentary on the Bible

Overview

of the

Old Testament

Dr. Charles R. Vogan Jr.

ISBN 978-0-6151-5618-7

Ravenbrook Publishers

A Subsidiary of
Shenandoah Bible Ministries

www.shenbible.org

Contents

Introduction

The Bible is a book to study. Like any textbook in other subject areas, the Bible is a sourcebook of data. It works with a very narrow field; it's about God and man – and their relationship. Unlike other textbooks, however, you don't need to move on to higher levels when you've mastered the basics of the Bible. The Word of God is deep enough to instruct the simple and the wise, the beginner and the master. Here you will find information from the Sunday School level to the collegiate level – and as far beyond that as you want to take it. There is no end to the depth of the knowledge of God.

For some reason there is a persuasion among scholarly circles that Bible study is a "devotional" act. Presumably we study the Bible during our "devotions," and one has an image of the dedicated Christian opening his Bible in the morning, before the day starts, and reading a chapter or two with a prayer to top it off. To tie that time of worship to the idea of Bible study, however, is an unfortunate misuse of the word "devotional." To me, a time of devotion brings up an image of the early Pietists who, appropriately enough, offered up their lives to God in prayer and "devoted" themselves to his will. Doing one's "devotions" is an act of submission to God.

But serious Bible study is like studying a physics textbook – which has nothing to do with "devotions." Picture a classroom, with teacher and students, and the assignment for the day, and a weekly test to make sure everyone is learning the lessons. The point of study is to *master the subject* – to learn a certain amount of data, to understand the lesson. Then when you've shown that you understand it, you move on to the next lesson – something related to it, something deeper, something that enlarges the picture that is forming in your mind.

This requires effort, of course. The "lazy man's" approach to Bible study is to simply read a little and close the book. We all know that this isn't *studying* it. We learned what studying was when we were in school. The students who studied are the ones who made the grade,

5

and they went on to college and successful careers. The students who didn't study usually ended up on the low end of society because they didn't have the skills necessary to fit into the more useful positions in the community.

Why study the Bible? Because Jesus is building a Kingdom, and he needs useful workers to help him. Bible study makes us skilled at doing the very tasks that make a church live and grow. The Lord uses people who know what's going on, and know how to glorify him.

The other side of this, of course, is that those who don't study the Bible end up being pretty useless to the Lord. They may take a part in the life of the church, but their ignorance and willfulness will end up wrecking things, not helping.

The starting point for all Christians, then, is to begin with the basics of the Bible. Unfortunately not every church, or church leader, understands how vital this step is for every believer. Often a church will take a new member under its wing and "nurture" them with sermons. That isn't studying. Try asking the average church member what the pastor preached about last week! Education experts tell us that we remember no more than 10% of what we hear. If sermons are the only thing that members are getting every Sunday, it's doubtful that they are learning much of anything.

What we have to do is set up a classroom environment and attack the Bible in a systematic way. It doesn't much matter what method you may use to do this – a classroom/homework model, a group working through the book – but a deliberate attempt to plunge into the Bible and master its teachings from beginning to end will go a long way to educating the members and making them useful workers in the church.

How much should we know about the Bible? It depends on how useful you want to be to the Lord and his work. Just as you might do with a worldly education, you can stop with a few basics and end up "sweeping floors" spiritually; more than that you won't be skilled to do, nor can you be trusted with critical jobs. And if you don't much care about how useful you are to the Lord, you'll probably stop way sooner than the rest of the class.

But if you're "devoted" completely to the Lord, you'll throw yourself into his textbook and learn as much as you can from it. You never know how or when he will choose to use you in his Kingdom. The committed Christian will lay his entire life before the Lord for his service and will not draw the line short.

Christ's Kingdom is huge, and there are many jobs to be done. Like the world, it consists of multiple levels. There is education, politics, food services, prisons and corrections, the military, business, community development, manufacturing, diplomacy, government – all this and more exists on the spiritual level. There are plenty of openings and much work to do. The point is that all of this requires skilled, educated, and dedicated labor to bring into a harmonious whole.

You no doubt remember someone – maybe it was you? – in school who declared, "I'll never use this stuff! Why do I have to learn it?" A child doesn't see the use in what he has to learn. An adult, however, has learned along the way that education prepares us for possibilities. We may not know where we will use it, but the need *will* come up, in unexpected places.

An adult also realizes the importance of taking part in the Kingdom. Unlike a child, who lives only for himself, a mature believer understands the need for helping others, for furthering the cause of Christ, for bringing glory to God. You don't need to tell him to take part in things; he knows why it's necessary. I'm describing a "spiritual adult," of course; there are many adults, unfortunately, in the church who are still "spiritual babies" who see no need at all for growing up and taking part in Christ's Kingdom.

All this is to introduce this Commentary on the Bible. Our purpose is to help the ordinary Christian understand God's Word – and to be able to use this knowledge for his own spiritual growth and helping out in Christ's Kingdom. It's not for scholars; you won't find the kind of "peripheral" subjects here that amuse philosophers and theologians. What you will get is a deeper understanding of God, and yourself in relation to him, to help you achieve your spiritual goals – and to help others also.

This material *will* help you achieve your spiritual goals. I have always assumed, and have found abundant proof of it, that the Bible is immensely useful to us. The more I study it, the more I wonder at how I did without it for so long! It has taken me *too* long to learn some of this material, due to many factors; but I wouldn't trade what I've learned for a world of riches. My goal here is to save you a lot of time and trouble – thirty years worth! – and speed up the learning process for you. It's not the end of the subject, but it will give you a significant head start on your own journey of learning at God's feet.

Again, we can never tell where God will use us in his Kingdom. So we aren't going to specialize in only one subject. You could call this a "liberal arts" education, meaning that you will learn the necessary aspects of many subjects in the Bible. You can specialize later on your own. Like any Liberal Arts program, the assumption is that you can hardly do without a general knowledge of the great sweep of the entire Bible. Cults, and deviant "ministries," almost always start up and thrive around ignorance of critical ideas in the Bible. These ideas are plainly taught there, but conveniently ignored by those being deceived by the devil.

My point is this: don't stop somewhere in, for example, Leviticus and proclaim, "I'll never need this!" Take my word for it – you will. Start in Genesis and work all the way through God's textbook to the book of Revelation. God wisely gave us all of it, and it requires a studious, balanced, and inquiring mind to see the whole picture that God is painting for us.

You may not see where things are going at the beginning, but I can help you there. We don't want you to get lost in the forest! I will give you certain "big picture" principles at the beginning that will help you see the direction of things in God's book. As you keep studying, you will find yourself learning things you didn't know, correcting false ideas that you had. Education has a way of doing that. Even in society, those who have little education are most prone to the superstitions and deceits of the world around them. The educated, however, have a clearer view of things and can make their way through problems and circumstances safely and profitably. Christians, too, survive better when they know what's going on.

> Then we will no longer be infants, tossed back and forth by the waves, and blown here and there by every wind of teaching and by the cunning and craftiness of men in their deceitful scheming. (Ephesians 4:14)

The Lord willing, we intend to work through every book in the Bible. In this volume – *Overview of the Old Testament* – we will focus on what is probably the average Christian's most problematic area of the Bible. It is my belief that *the entire Bible* is God's Word to his Church. The Old Testament is where we will get 95% of our Christian faith – yes, it's that important. If churches and Christians are struggling in our day, it's largely because they hardly ever look at the Old Testament, let alone take it seriously. Effective Christian workers will be able to use the Old Testament as well as the New to build God's Kingdom, as Jesus once told us.

> Therefore every teacher of the Law who has been instructed about the kingdom of Heaven is like the owner of a house who brings out of his storeroom new treasures as well as old. (Matthew 13:52)

So, let's begin.

Introduction

General background
on the Bible

Some Background on the Bible Itself

There is a problem with the Bible.

Most people don't realize that there *is* a problem with the Bible. We have had a Bible for all of our lives, and probably never wondered where it came from. It was here before any of us were born, and will be here when we all die and the next generation arrives. It seems so unchanging, so much a part of our tradition, that it hardly ever occurs to us that there might be real problems with it!

But there *are* problems — which is plain to see if you listen to what people say about the Bible. For example, many times people argue about which version of the Bible to use. Did you know that this argument isn't just over personal preferences? The real problem is that those versions are based on different Bible texts! The translators picked which Greek and Hebrew texts to work from, which leads to many of the variations that we have in our versions today.

Another problem is that the Bible didn't just drop out of Heaven one day, ready-made, in its present form. It came about over thousands of years, in pieces here and there, and went through many hands in the process. In other words, the Bible grew and developed over a long time. The books were written in response to individual needs and circumstances, in cultures strange to us, originally for their use, not ours! What are we to think about a book that developed in this way?

However, the most serious problem about the Bible is this: ***We do not have the original Bible.*** Whatever scrolls or parchments that the Biblical authors wrote their books on were lost long ago. The Bibles that we have today are based on copies of copies of copies, and nobody really knows how much or how little those copies deviated from the original written books.

These are some of the serious problems in the area of Bible research, and they have naturally resulted in arguments over which

Bible version to use. Most people, as I mentioned, never knew that such problems existed! Yet they become caught up in the arguments over versions too, often arguing for one or the other with no knowledge of the real issues involved.

What we want to do in this study is learn some of the history of the Bible — in non-technical language — so that we can make intelligent decisions about how to use the Bible. What we will find is that God has preserved his Word in a miraculous way. In spite of the problems, we still have a book that we can trust. It is still the Word of God, sufficient to save us and reveal the truth about God and ourselves.

The Written Word

"In the beginning was the Word, and the Word was with God, and the Word was God." (John 1:1) When God speaks, that is Jesus Christ. Christ is God's message to the world for our salvation and his glory. That's why it is so important to trust in everything Jesus says to us and everything that he does for us. "For no matter how many promises God has made, they are 'Yes' in Christ." (2 Corinthians 1:20)

But there are two levels to the Word of God. Jesus is the *living* Word, and the Bible is the *written* Word. God's truth is life, but it is also information that we need to know and act upon. A person who has the life of Christ in him (through the Spirit) literally feeds upon the truth of the Bible, and grows spiritually as a result. "...The new self, which is being renewed in *knowledge* in the image of its Creator." (Colossians 3:10) "Be transformed by the renewing of your *mind*." (Romans 12:2)

At first the only Word of God was the spoken Word. In Genesis 1 we read about God creating the world through his Word, and in Genesis 2-3 he spoke to Adam and Eve about obedience and sin and death. But it wasn't long until those words were written down. Scholars have found that writing existed since the dawn of civilization, and the records of the earth's first generations were probably written on tablets long before Moses collected the stories together for his books.

14

Why does God want these things written? Why does he attach so much importance to the written Word? *First*, to preserve the words for future generations. The people to whom God first spoke needed to hear his truth, but they weren't the only ones who needed to hear it! That truth applies to all men and women of all ages. Since God chose not to speak directly from Heaven to every human being, he put it in a book for us to study and learn.

Second, writing something down makes it permanent and unchanging. If we only depended on what people tell us, the story would get changed from generation to generation. Someone would forget a detail, or change something that he doesn't like, or add new "truths" that weren't there before. So instead of submitting his truth to the whims of man, God decided to write it down, first on stone tablets and then on paper. This is a form that can't be changed so easily.

So, what we have now is the eternal truth of God in a book. The Bible tells us who God really is, who we really are, and what we must do to be saved from the spiritual danger that we are in. There is no other source for this information. It's extremely important that we both learn and trust in what it says.

But, as is true with everything that man is involved in, there are certain problems with the Bible. For example, though the Church is the body of Christ, we certainly don't see the perfect holiness of Christ in each member of the Church! There are many problems that ought not to be in the Church; however, they are due not to the Lord but to our own sin and ignorance. The same is true with the Bible. God spoke the pure truth to men in the past, but what we have now in our Bibles is tainted with the sins and ignorance of men as they handled the Word of God.

Many people, when they learn about these problems, decide not to believe the Bible anymore. Why should they depend on a book with mistakes in it? We are going to take a different approach here, however. We have to learn to distinguish between man's works and God's works, and put our trust in what God does regardless of what man does. Just as we can't discount Christ because of the sins of a particular Christian, we can't discount the trustworthiness of the Bible

15

because of some problems that exist in translations. What God gave us in his Word is "perfect, reviving the soul." (Psalm 19:7) We just have to work around the imperfections that man introduced into it.

The most serious problem that we have with the Bible, however, is that the original documents — the actual scrolls that Moses and David and the Prophets and the apostles wrote — no longer exist. We don't know what happened to them. Perhaps they were kept for a long time — certainly they were copied, in order to preserve the writing — but now they are gone. Those original manuscripts are called the **autographs**, because they were written by the authors themselves. Christians believe that those autographs were the very words of God, as he directed the authors to write them. And since they are the Word of God, they would have been pure and accurate, without error of any kind. But we can't say that about the copies that men made of them, as we shall see shortly.

History of the Old Testament

Technically, Adam was the first man that God spoke to. So the Bible dates back to the beginning of human history, something that no other "sacred" literature of other religions can claim. And in that first encounter we also learn what Holy Scriptures really consist of: they are the words of God, directed to man, revealing the nature of God to us (something that we would otherwise not know) and revealing what we must to do please him.

How do we come to have those first words of God? Did Adam write them down? Probably he remembered them and told them to his children, who told them to their children — and on it went through the family. That's called "oral tradition," when the elders preserve the memory of the past by telling stories to the young. But their storytelling wasn't like ours. They remembered *exactly* how the story went, word for word, and didn't change a thing in it when they retold it. There was an art to storytelling in those days, and not everyone could do it. Even after being retold generations later, you could trust in the fact that the story was told in exactly the same words that the ancient generations told it. In this respect the storytellers were "living books" who were passing on the tradition.

But we also know that it was likely that the events in the early Genesis stories were written down fairly soon in the history of man. Cuneiform (*pronounce*: kyou-NEE-i-form) tablets from ancient cultures have been found dating from before 3000 BC! Cuneiform was an alphabet/language that served for thousands of years in ancient civilizations; one used a stick with a wedge-shaped tip to press marks into soft clay, and then the clay was baked to harden it into tablets that could literally last for thousands of years. What did people write on cuneiform tablets? Business matters, political announcements, personal letters —the same kinds of things that we write about in our own day. This means two things: that writing was something that trained people in almost any early culture could do, and it was a common thing to do. And that means that the history of the beginning of the world would have certainly been recorded on tablets by somebody in Adam's line.

There is another evidence that Moses worked from written records when he wrote the history of Genesis. (Remember that Moses' own story didn't start until Exodus; when he wrote Genesis, he was not recording what he had seen – only what passed down to him through tradition and what the Spirit revealed to him directly.) If you look carefully you will notice the phrase "This is the account of ..." (or in the KJV it says "These are the generations of ...") in several places throughout the book — it separates one section from another. (See Genesis 5:1; 6:9; 10:1; 11:10, etc.) This was a characteristic way of winding up a story on a *clay tablet*, a sort of conclusion that the writer added at the bottom of the tablet. It also served to tie together several tablets into single story, so that a person wouldn't get confused about which tablet to look at next (we do the same thing when we number our pages in a book). Existing cuneiform tablets use this technique, so it's interesting to see evidence in the Genesis record that Moses used tablets.

At any rate, Moses was the one who gathered the available records and created the beginning of our Bible. But we mustn't forget one important point: the Spirit of God was directing Moses as to what to write. Doubtless there were large parts of the story to fill in that weren't in the written records that were available to him – such as what exactly happened at the Creation. At those points the Spirit revealed the truth to Moses so that he would know the right message to record. Peter tells us that prophets never made anything up when they wrote the Word of God:

> Above all, you must understand that no prophecy of Scripture came about by the prophet's own interpretation. For prophecy never had its origin in the will of man, but men spoke from God as they were carried along by the Holy Spirit. (2 Peter 1:20-21)

Moses, being the greatest of the Old Testament prophets, would certainly have been faithful to the witness of the Spirit as he wrote his books.

Moses probably knew several languages; remember that he was educated in Pharaoh's court and would have had opportunity to learn many things. He probably knew cuneiform (a universal language in those days), Egyptian, and Hebrew. Hebrew he would have learned from his own people, the Israelites. He would need to know cuneiform in order to copy the old records for his new Bible.

When the Lord wrote the Ten Commandments on stone tablets, he probably wrote it in an old type of script — not in the kind of Hebrew letters that we are familiar with today. But if you ever see the Ten Commandments in standard Hebrew (for example, in a synagogue), this is what it would look like (this is from Exodus 20:1-17):

וַיְדַבֵּר אֱלֹהִים אֵת כָּל־הַדְּבָרִים
הָאֵלֶּה לֵאמֹר׃ ס
2 אָנֹכִי יְהוָה אֱלֹהֶיךָ אֲשֶׁר הוֹצֵאתִיךָ מֵאֶרֶץ מִצְרַיִם
מִבֵּית עֲבָדִים׃
3 לֹא יִהְיֶה־לְךָ אֱלֹהִים אֲחֵרִים עַל־פָּנָיַ׃
4 לֹא תַעֲשֶׂה־לְךָ פֶסֶל וְכָל־תְּמוּנָה אֲשֶׁר בַּשָּׁמַיִם
מִמַּעַל וַאֲשֶׁר בָּאָרֶץ מִתַּחַת וַאֲשֶׁר בַּמַּיִם מִתַּחַת לָאָרֶץ׃
5 לֹא־תִשְׁתַּחֲוֶה לָהֶם וְלֹא תָעָבְדֵם כִּי אָנֹכִי יְהוָה
אֱלֹהֶיךָ אֵל קַנָּא פֹּקֵד עֲוֹן אָבֹת עַל־בָּנִים עַל־שִׁלֵּשִׁים
וְעַל־רִבֵּעִים לְשֹׂנְאָי׃

6 וְעֹ֤שֶׂה חֶ֙סֶד֙ לַאֲלָפִ֔ים לְאֹהֲבַ֖י וּלְשֹׁמְרֵ֥י מִצְוֺתָֽי: ס

7 לֹ֥א תִשָּׂ֛א אֶת־שֵֽׁם־יְהוָ֥ה אֱלֹהֶ֖יךָ לַשָּׁ֑וְא כִּ֣י לֹ֤א יְנַקֶּה֙ יְהוָ֔ה אֵ֛ת אֲשֶׁר־יִשָּׂ֥א אֶת־שְׁמ֖וֹ לַשָּֽׁוְא: ף

8 זָכ֛וֹר אֶת־י֥וֹם הַשַּׁבָּ֖ת לְקַדְּשֽׁוֹ:

9 שֵׁ֤שֶׁת יָמִים֙ תַּֽעֲבֹ֔ד וְעָשִׂ֖יתָ כָּל־מְלַאכְתֶּֽךָ:

10 וְי֙וֹם֙ הַשְּׁבִיעִ֔י שַׁבָּ֖ת לַיהוָ֣ה אֱלֹהֶ֑יךָ לֹֽא־תַעֲשֶׂ֣ה כָל־מְלָאכָ֡ה אַתָּ֣ה וּבִנְךָֽ־וּ֠בִתֶּךָ עַבְדְּךָ֨ וַאֲמָֽתְךָ֜ וּבְהֶמְתֶּ֗ךָ וְגֵרְךָ֖ אֲשֶׁ֥ר בִּשְׁעָרֶֽיךָ:

11 כִּ֣י שֵֽׁשֶׁת־יָמִים֩ עָשָׂ֨ה יְהוָ֜ה אֶת־הַשָּׁמַ֣יִם וְאֶת־הָאָ֗רֶץ אֶת־הַיָּם֙ וְאֶת־כָּל־אֲשֶׁר־בָּ֔ם וַיָּ֖נַח בַּיּ֣וֹם הַשְּׁבִיעִ֑י עַל־כֵּ֗ן בֵּרַ֧ךְ יְהוָ֛ה אֶת־י֥וֹם הַשַּׁבָּ֖ת וַֽיְקַדְּשֵֽׁהוּ: ס

12 כַּבֵּ֥ד אֶת־אָבִ֖יךָ וְאֶת־אִמֶּ֑ךָ לְמַ֙עַן֙ יַאֲרִכ֣וּן יָמֶ֔יךָ עַ֚ל הָֽאֲדָמָ֔ה אֲשֶׁר־יְהוָ֥ה אֱלֹהֶ֖יךָ נֹתֵ֥ן לָֽךְ: ס

13 לֹ֥א תִּרְצָֽח: ס

14 לֹ֥א תִּנְאָֽף: ס

15 לֹ֥א תִּגְנֹֽב: ס

16 לֹֽא־תַעֲנֶ֥ה בְרֵעֲךָ֖ עֵ֥ד שָֽׁקֶר: ס

17 לֹ֥א תַחְמֹ֖ד בֵּ֣ית רֵעֶ֑ךָ לֹֽא־תַחְמֹ֞ד אֵ֣שֶׁת רֵעֶ֗ךָ וְעַבְדּ֤וֹ וַאֲמָתוֹ֙ וְשׁוֹר֣וֹ וַחֲמֹר֔וֹ וְכֹ֖ל אֲשֶׁ֥ר לְרֵעֶֽךָ: ף

(By the way, Hebrew reads from right to left, and the front of the book is what we call the back of the book. This is common for most oriental languages.)

But Moses didn't give us only the Ten Commandments. He wrote (as we have seen) the old records from before his time (the book of Genesis), the new commandments from Mt. Sinai, and everything else that God spoke to him throughout his long ministry with the Israelites. In fact, Deuteronomy (his last book) ends with his death at the border of the land of Canaan (an event written presumably by his successor!). All five of his books are called the **Torah** (which means, in Hebrew, "The Law"). Since the work of Moses consisted of the calling, creation, and government of the people of Israel, the Torah is their most prized possession and by far the most important part of their Bible. These are the books of the Torah:

The Torah:

Genesis
Exodus
Leviticus
Numbers
Deuteronomy

The rest of the Old Testament is actually only a commentary and explanation of the Torah, as far as the Jews are concerned. The Jews divided up their Bible into three sections: the Torah, the Prophets, and the Writings. The **Prophets** included these books:

Former Prophets:

Joshua
Judges
1-2 Samuel
1-2 Kings

Latter Prophets:

Isaiah
Jeremiah
Ezekiel

The Twelve (Minor) Prophets:

Hosea	**Nahum**
Joel	**Habakkuk**
Amos	**Zephaniah**
Obadiah	**Haggai**
Jonah	**Zechariah**
Micah	**Malachi**

The **Writings**, which contained all the rest of the books, was the third section and of third importance to the Jews. The following books made up the Writings:

The Writings:

Psalms	Lamentations
Job	Esther
Proverbs	Daniel
Ruth	Ezra
Song of Songs	Nehemiah
Ecclesiastes	1-2 Chronicles

All the books of the Old Testament were written by the time Jesus was born. In fact, Malachi was the last prophet to write a book that made it into the Old Testament Scriptures. (The Apocrypha is a set of books by additional writers since the time of Malachi; they never made it into the Bible principally because God didn't reveal this material through prophets in their time — which made it doubtful that they were really revelation from God. True revelation is always connected with a prophet.)

When the Christian Church rearranged the books of the Old Testament, it chose a time-table approach instead of a prophet-based approach. The books that were written earliest — Moses' books — come first, then the historical books, and then the major books in the Writings section — Psalms and the Wisdom books — and then the prophets. It pretty much follows the *history* of the Old Testament in its order.

Though the Jews had settled on which books made up their Holy Scriptures by the time of Christ, one problem that remained was vowels. Early Hebrew didn't have any vowels in it. It's as if we would write the previous sentence like this: **rly Hbrw ddnt hv ny vwls n t.** We have a little problem reading this kind of thing, and when the Jews no longer used Hebrew as the common language they started having problems too. They forgot what the vowels for some of the words were! So before the problem got completely out of hand, a group of scholars called the Masoretes worked for several hundred years devising a vowel system for the text of the Hebrew Bible. They decided that the text was too sacred to change — and inserting new vowels between the consonants *would* be a change. So they invented marks to put above and below the consonants which would represent vowels. Here is a word without and with its vowels:

האדמה   —   h'dmh

הָאֲדָמָה   —   hā' ^ad āmāh

You don't have to know Hebrew to see that the second word has additional marks below it. Those are some of the vowels that the Masoretes invented. The text that they finalized, therefore, is called the Masoretic Text and was completed about 900 AD.

The oldest existing manuscript that we have now (besides the Dead Sea Scrolls, which we will look at below) is the one kept in St. Petersburg, Russia (of all places!) – the Leningrad Codex. It was copied in 1008 AD by a scholar in the Ben Asher family (famous for their scribes). It is the basis of many of our present translations of the Old Testament.

History of the New Testament

Jesus came as the living Word of God (John 1:1), and he revealed the truth of God to us so that we might be saved. The words of Jesus themselves became the written Word for us.

He spoke in Aramaic, because that's what all the Jews of his time used as their common tongue. We're pretty sure he knew Hebrew, but he wouldn't have had to know it in order to read the Scriptures — they had already been translated into Aramaic.

An interesting detail that reveals the mix of languages in their culture is the account of the sign posted on top of Jesus' cross:

> Pilate had a notice prepared and fastened to the cross. It read: JESUS OF NAZARETH, THE KING OF THE JEWS. Many of the Jews read this sign, for the place where Jesus was crucified was near the city, and the sign was written in Aramaic, Latin and Greek. (John 19:19-20)

It was an era of empires, and business flourished between widespread cultures. It was natural for everyone to know at least two languages (as is true in Europe today, for example).

God times his works so that they will have the greatest possible effect. In this case, the Gospel came at one of the critical times of human history: never before could the message of the Gospel spread so rapidly and easily from one end of the civilized world to the other, and the common languages had a lot to do with that.

The disciples, charged with the task of carrying the news of Jesus to the world, naturally wrote their books in the language that the most people would understand: Greek. And they didn't use classical Greek, the language of the poets and theater and upper society. They used the Greek that the common man on the street would understand — "vulgar" or common Greek, what we know today as **Koine** (*pronounce*: COIN-ay) Greek. They took these Scriptures and taught them to farmers, milkmaids, blacksmiths, housewives, slaves, and other "lower class" people who would understand the message and, by faith, receive it.

At times we find a fascinating interplay of languages in the text that, if we only work with English, we would miss. For example, the story of Jesus questioning Peter about his love for him (John 21:15-18) was written in Greek, by the apostle John. But Jesus and Peter originally had this discussion in *Aramaic*. In Aramaic there is only one commonly used word for "love"; but in Greek there are two — "phileo" (brotherly, friendly love) and "agape" (self-denying love). In John's account, he shows that Jesus asked if Peter had "agape" love for him, and Peter said that he did have "phileo" love for him. Since there was only one Aramaic word that they both used, John is using the different Greek words to show us what each speaker *meant*. With this

linguistic trick, he reveals to us the true state of Peter's heart —
something that we wouldn't have known otherwise if we had listened in
on the original conversation. The trouble is that John's revelation gets
lost on modern English readers – because we also have only one word
for "love."

This is a portion of John's Gospel, written in Greek (this is John
1:1-5):

Ἐν ἀρχῇ ἦν ὁ λόγος, καὶ ὁ λόγος ἦν πρὸς τὸν θεόν, καὶ θεὸς
ἦν ὁ λόγος.

2 οὗτος ἦν ἐν ἀρχῇ πρὸς τὸν θεόν.

3 πάντα δι᾽ αὐτοῦ ἐγένετο, καὶ χωρὶς αὐτοῦ ἐγένετο οὐδὲ ἕν. ὃ
γέγονεν

4 ἐν αὐτῷ ζωὴ ἦν, καὶ ἡ ζωὴ ἦν τὸ φῶς τῶν ἀνθρώπων·

5 καὶ τὸ φῶς ἐν τῇ σκοτίᾳ φαίνει, καὶ ἡ σκοτία αὐτὸ οὐ
κατέλαβεν.

Two of the Gospels (Matthew and John) were written by original
disciples (that is, men given in the "official" list of disciples who first
followed Jesus — Matthew 10:2-4, Mark 3:16-19, and Luke 6:13-16).
Mark was a follower of Peter, and therefore he got his stories from an
eyewitness. Luke was a follower of Paul, but he also collected
information from eyewitnesses:

> Many have undertaken to draw up an account of the
> things that have been fulfilled among us, just as they
> were handed down to us by those who from the first
> were eyewitnesses and servants of the Word. Therefore,
> since I myself have carefully investigated everything
> from the beginning, it seemed good also to me to write
> an orderly account for you, most excellent Theophilus,
> so that you may know the certainty of the things you
> have been taught. (Luke 1:1-4)

This illustrates a very important point about the books of the New
Testament: this information came from men who saw and heard Jesus
Christ when he lived on earth. This is special testimony, therefore,
something that the Church has never had since then. What they tell us

about him is the foundation of our faith, the standard of truth about him. It is for good reason that Paul says we are —

> ... fellow citizens with God's people and members of God's household, *built on the foundation of the apostles and prophets*, with Christ Jesus himself as the chief cornerstone. (Ephesians 2:19-20)

We are not allowed to deviate from the apostolic writings in our faith. Therefore their writings are critical to us.

Most of the books of the New Testament were really intended as letters, sent to congregations around the Roman Empire. The Epistles, for example, are obviously personal letters to churches. But you can be sure that these letters became prized property; everyone would want a copy of their own to study and meditate on. In fact, churches would hear about a particular letter that one church had received, and request a copy for themselves. Soon there were many copies of the New Testament letters circulating everywhere.

The Canon

The initial excitement of Christ's life and resurrection produced shock waves in the Roman Empire. People from all walks of life, even some of the imperial family, became believers. Churches sprang up everywhere, converts numbered in the tens of thousands, and of course everyone wanted to hear and see the stories about Jesus.

This produced a market for written material. Soon there were other books appearing besides the ones that the apostles themselves wrote. Some of them were simply sermons and lessons on the life of the Lord, but some were, unfortunately, false Gospels written by impostors. Some of them had ridiculous stories in them and they weren't hard to judge as false (one of them told the story of Jesus, as a child, making birds out of clay and then breathing life into them!). Others looked like they might be genuine and caused a lot of confusion in the Church. Which books were they supposed to believe in?

The situation got so bad that the leaders in the Church decided to hold meetings to determine what books (out of the hundreds that existed) God wanted them to call Scripture and what books were only productions of men. After a lot of discussion, in 367 AD they finally came up with an authoritative list — which they called the **canon** of Scripture. This list of books is what makes up our Bibles today. You may be interested in knowing that they argued long over whether several books should be in the canon — for example, James, Jude, 2 Peter, and 2 and 3 John. (If you remember, Martin Luther, as late as 1500 AD, himself wondered whether the book of James should be in the canon!)

Their rule was this: they would include whatever books claimed (and proved) apostolic authorship. Usually a letter had the apostle's name on it, sometimes tradition proved that it came from a certain apostle, and sometimes there was internal evidence in the letters themselves (for example, Peter's testimony of Paul's writings in 2 Peter 3:15-16). But that still leaves a couple of doubtful books, most notably Hebrews (which is still a point of argument in our day!) since it doesn't say who wrote it. So they also used some spiritual sense and included any book that obviously had divine authority in its message. That effectively eliminated most of the books that were circulating then, good and bad, and forever designated the books that we have now as the New Testament Scriptures.

The Old Testament canon was decided by the Jews about 70 AD, which was really only an official statement about what they had long since agreed upon. Someone once said that we have a better authority for the canon of the Old Testament than we have for the New Testament — Jesus himself, along with his apostles, used these books as the Holy Scriptures in their Gospel preaching.

Preserving the Truth

People wanted to record information permanently long before they had such exotic materials as paper and copier machines and computers and printing presses. So they had to use whatever was available in their low-technology world.

The first types of writing were done on stone, both by painting and carving. Since carving lasts almost forever, this was the method of choice. It was slow going to take hammer and chisel and carve out pictures and letters, and one could only fit so much on a large stone before having to continue on another stone. But it was so durable that we still have stone tablets that were carved thousands of years ago.

By the way, one theory about why Hebrew was written from right to left is this: imagine that you have a stone tablet to carve, and you have a hammer and chisel to do it with. It is much easier to use the hammer in your right hand and chisel to the left than the other way around (unless you are left-handed, which few people are!). Since writing started out this way, it's probable that this accounts for the direction of early alphabets.

But the disadvantages of carving in stone forced creative people to find new ways of writing. One popular method was **cuneiform** (kyoo-NEE-i-form) writing, in which one uses a stick with a wedge-shaped tip to press marks into soft clay. Then when the tablet is complete, bake it in an oven to make it almost as hard as stone. Cuneiform looks something like this:

Another way of writing was with **papyrus** (*pronounce*: pa-PIE-rus), a plant that grew along marshes and rivers. They would slit the stems and lay them down in rows, then glue on another layer crossways to the first layer. It was actually the beginnings of the paper industry. Then they made a black ink with water and charcoal and used a pointed stick to write on the papyrus sheets. The sheets didn't last as long as clay tablets, but they were much easier to handle and were, of course, much lighter. They could also store more of them in a smaller space.

A third way of writing was to use scraped sheep-skin as a sort of paper. Another name for this material was **parchment**.

In order to solve the problem of storing their writings, they invented two ways of putting the material together. One was the **scroll**, in which the sheepskin or papyrus was made into a long strip, the message written on it, and then (starting at one end) they rolled the strip into a tight roll. With a scroll they could store a lot of information in a small space, and it was easy to carry around. The major problem was finding the text they wanted — they had to unroll most or all of the scroll to locate the spot!

A second way to assemble the material was in a **codex** — what we call a book. They cut sheets out of papyrus or sheepskin and glued them together along one edge, so that it formed individual pages. This was the most efficient way to do it, since all the information was easily found (not like a scroll). The only drawbacks were that it was a little bulkier to handle, and the pages could come apart over time.

Until the invention of the printing press around 1450 AD, making books was an extremely tedious affair: they were all copied by hand. This means that one person could make only one book at a time. "Libraries", therefore, in the old days were small and very rare.

The Jews were almost paranoid about how they copied their Scriptures. The text was so sacred to them that they did everything they could think of to keep mistakes from happening. In God's providence, this was so helpful for preserving the Hebrew Bible, since it had to survive the hand of man for twice the time that the New Testament did. Remember that the first books of Moses were penned about 1500 BC! Thus we have a book that is 3500 years old. It's a good thing that the Jews took their copying so seriously.

For example, each scribe had to check his work against the standard during the entire copying process. When he was done, he had additional checks to do in order to insure its accuracy. They knew how many words and how many letters were supposed to be in each book of the Old Testament. They knew how many times each letter of the alphabet was used in each book. They even knew where the middle word and the middle *letter* of the Old Testament was! If a copy checked out to this degree of perfection, then they allowed its use; otherwise they either corrected it or threw it away and started over.

They were jealous for the integrity of the Scriptures, and sometimes their zealousness frustrates us who would like to see some of those ancient documents. One thing that they did was this: when they were done making a new copy of the Bible, they would destroy the old copy so that it wouldn't suffer from unholy wear and tear from continued use. It is this that accounts for the fact that we have very few ancient manuscripts of the Old Testament now. There are only a few hundred full and partial copies of the Old Testament in existence; in comparison, there are thousands of full and partial manuscripts of the New Testament in existence.

Another characteristic of Old Testament manuscripts is that they used no vowels at all, as we previously saw. When everyone spoke Hebrew this was no problem, since Hebrew doesn't rely on vowels as heavily as English does. But sometimes it is a bit confusing to someone who doesn't know Hebrew well; and by the time of Jesus, when only the scholars knew it well, people were a little worried about those vowels — they were beginning to forget what they were!

The New Testament, written in Greek, had vowels in it — it resembles English much more than Hebrew does. One bothersome characteristic (to us, anyway!) of many of their early manuscripts was that THEY WROTE EVERYTHING IN CAPITAL LETTERS ONLY — these copies were called "uncials." In "minuscule" manuscripts they at least used small letters as we do. But the major problem of early Greek manuscripts is that they used no punctuation! No periods, commas, question marks, quotes — nothing. And some of them didn't even put spaces between the words! Sometimes it is nearly impossible to determine how to break up a sentence, or even where one sentence stops and the next one starts! A well-known example of this is in John 1:3-4 —

Here? *or* **Here?**

καί χωρίς αὐτοῦ ἐγένετο οὐδέ ἕν ὃ γέγονεν ἐν αὐτῷ ζωή ἦν,

You can translate this in one of two ways, and both ways make sense: either it says, *"**and without him nothing was made. That**"* *which came to be in him was life*," or you can translate it as "*and without him nothing was made that has been made. In him was life.*" Most modern translations choose the second option, but it could just as easily be translated the first way too. (The Greek Bible that most people use, for example, prefers to punctuate it the first way.) Without punctuation there is no way we can be certain of it.

One more thing you should know. The system of verse numbers and chapter numbers is a (relatively) modern invention. The books were not first written with the verses numbered. They were letters and histories, and of course the writers never thought to break up the text like we do. The verse numbers were added to the Old Testament about 900 AD by Masorete scholars, and later to the New Testament by a Catholic scholar (some say that he did it while he was on horseback during his travels, which may account for the uneven and strange way he assigned some of the verses!).

Copying Problems

We moderns take our handy inventions for granted. When we want a copy of something, all we have to do is use a copier and we get an exact image (spots and all!) of the original in seconds. People in ancient times would have loved to own a copier! They, unfortunately, had to do it the old-fashioned way: by hand.

There were several ways to attack the problem. One was to assign someone the job of making a duplicate of a particular manuscript. He would work for months, painstakingly copying every letter and mark, producing a single exact duplicate from the original. As you can imagine, it was too easy to make a mistake. The sheer tedium of that much copying would likely produce errors. For example, these are the kinds of errors that can happen:

> ♦ *Duplicate words* — After copying for hours, one can get pretty tired and the words start blurring together in weary eyes. It's easy to get distracted and then, coming back to your work, think that you haven't yet copied the last word that you read in the original — when really you have already copied it.

♦ *Missing words* — The opposite problem from the last one and also easy to do. You may think that you already copied the word and go on, when really you are skipping it.

♦ *Duplicate lines* — If you follow along in the original by keeping your finger on the line that you are copying, it's easy to imagine forgetting to move your finger down a line — which means that you will end up copying the same line twice.

♦ *Missing lines* — The opposite problem from the last one and even easier to do, since you could move your finger down the page too far and miss an entire line in the process.

♦ *Misspelled words* — Instead of writing the word exactly as it is spelled, someone could read the word and then unthinkingly write the word with a different spelling — especially if the writer has always misspelled that word in the past.

♦ *Switched letters* — This happened a lot. The writer simply swapped two letters around. It's as if we would write "owe" instead of "woe." The trouble is that in Hebrew there are a lot of words that turn into other valid words simply by switching letters around. So this kind of mistake is hard to catch.

The point is that these mistakes aren't things that *could* have happened, they *did* happen. We can see many examples of them in old manuscripts. You would think that they are so obvious that a good copyist would have avoided them; but remember that not all copyists were good at their work, and in the middle of a tedious task you aren't thinking about whether what you are writing makes sense — you are just writing the letters in a mechanical way.

Another way to produce a copy is to gather a team of copyists into a room and have one person read the original out loud. Then each copyist would write down what he heard. If you have ten copyists, you would have ten copies made at the same time. This is a much more efficient way of producing many copies! The problem is that it leads to a new set of errors that can and often did happen:

♦ *Homonyms* — A homonym is a word that sounds like another word, but it is spelled differently because it is a different word. For instance, the words "reign" and "rain" are homonyms. You can easily imagine how a copyist would hear one word and write another by mistake.

♦ *Missed words* — If you aren't looking at the original copy yourself, it may be difficult to catch all the words that the reader speaks. It would be easy to leave out a word or two.

There were two more problems that came up during copying that led to errors in manuscripts. The first was that, especially while copying the New Testament books, sometimes the copyist himself was not a Christian and therefore wasn't very concerned with the accuracy of what he was doing. A Christian has a keener sense of the importance of God's Word and being faithful in its transmission; to an unbeliever, it was just a job, and accuracy wasn't a matter of faith to him.

The second problem was that sometimes a later editor would "fix" what he thought was certainly an error in the text, when really there was nothing wrong with it. He thought that an earlier copyist made a mistake, and he would insert the "correction" into the text itself or write it in the margin for the benefit of future copyists. Thus a new error was born. The most famous example of this was Judges 18:30. The editor was aghast that the text said that the evil priest who led idol worship at Dan was a grandson of Moses, the man of God! Not wanting to let Moses' reputation be ruined, he inserted the letter **N** (Hebrew נ) to make the name Moses read Manasseh (remember that Hebrew didn't have vowels, so he didn't have to add them).

↓

מֹשֶׁה   became   מְנַשֶׁה

It just so happens, however, that the priest *was* a descendant of Moses. But the change got into every copy of the Hebrew Bible since then. See for yourself!

When someone made a mistake in a copy that nobody was aware of, you can see what would happen. If, in the future, someone made another copy of that one, the second would have the same error in it that the first one had. For example, we can imagine something like the following happening in a chain of copies:

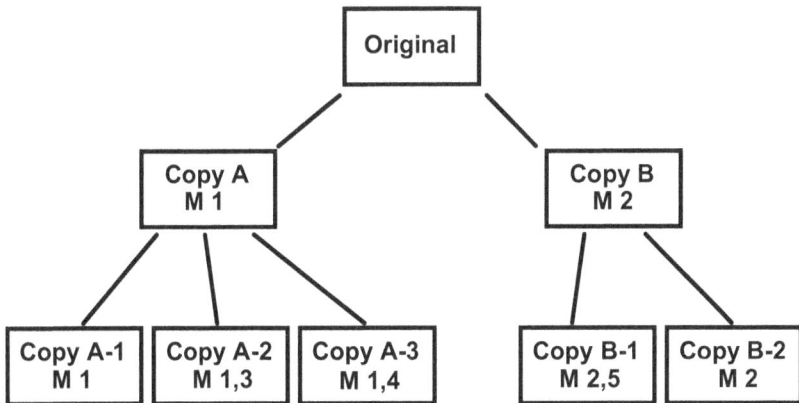

Figure 1 – Manuscript families

Let's say that someone made two copies of the **Original** and sent them to two different cities: **Copy A** and **Copy B**. The problem is that **Copy A** had a mistake in it — **M1** — and **Copy B** had a different mistake in it — **M2**. Then each church in each city decided to make additional copies. From **Copy A** came **Copy A-1**, **Copy A-2**, and **Copy A-3** — all of which have the same mistake **M1** in them. And in the process of copying, **Copy A-2** picked up an additional mistake **M3** and **Copy A-3** has a mistake **M4**. Meanwhile, in the second church, they made **Copy B-1** and **Copy B-2** from their copy. And **Copy B-1** got a new error **M5**.

As more copies are made, each "family" of copies develop new errors and preserve the old errors that are distinctive to that family. Pretty soon you could tell where a copy was made simply by checking what kind of errors were in the text!

To give you an idea of the kinds of problems that translators have to consider, here is a sample of what is at the bottom of a particular page in our Greek Bible:

---

[7] **33** {D} *ἡμῖν* 142 // *ἡμῶν* p[74] ℵ A B C* D ψ it[ar,c,d,t] vg eth Hilary Ambrose Cosmos // *αὐτῶν* 629 it[gig] cop[sa,bo.mss] Ambrose // *αὐτῶν ἡμῖν* C[3] E P 049 056 0142 33 81 88 104 181 326 330 436 451 614 630 945 1241 1505 1739 1877 2127 2412 2492 2495 *Byz Lect*[m] *l*[1443] it[e] (syr[p,h]) arm geo Chrysostom Cosmos Greek[acc.to] [Bede] Theophylact // *omit* cop[bo.mss]

It's a footnote for Acts 13:33. The problem is whether to translate it "*... he has fulfilled for us, their children*" or "*... he has fulfilled for us, the children.*" The first two sets, and the fourth set, of manuscripts (the // marks separate the sets) *do* have the word "their", and the rest of them *don't* — they just have various forms of the word "for us." The last one omits the entire phrase and makes it read "for the children". (The numbers represent individual manuscripts — they can keep track of them better that way.) Which manuscripts are right? The "D" at the beginning is the scale of difficulty in trying to decide what the correct reading is. Since there are *very* dependable manuscripts that disagree here, the scholars could only make an educated guess about which one to use. If they had put "A", this means that all the good manuscripts agree on a certain reading and the less dependable manuscripts disagree. "B" and "C" would mean there is more doubt about it.

This should give you an idea about how difficult it is for translators and Greek scholars to discover how the original autographs really read. But it also shows you the nature of the problem: none of the variations are about points of doctrine, or things that should divide Christians. Fortunately, the Bible is the best preserved document in all of history; in comparison, other ancient books, like Homer's stories, vary so widely from copy to copy that you would think that they were almost two different stories!

Manuscript Families

The "civilized world" at the time of the apostles was the Roman Empire, stretching all the way around the Mediterranean Sea. Christian teachers and preachers found it easy to use Rome's roads and communication network to spread the Gospel all over the Empire. Churches sprang up all over the place, but there were certain churches that were in major metropolitan areas and therefore drew the most Christians and — important to our discussion here — potential scholars.

Here is a map of the eastern end of the Empire, with major centers of learning:

Figure 2 – Manuscript Families

The apostles worked originally from Jerusalem, and spread out from there to other cities. Their letters spread out too, and as each church received an apostolic letter they got busy producing copies for everyone who wanted one. Soon there were large collections of letters in each city, laboriously but lovingly copied from the original. We call these collections by city **families of manuscripts**.

We have already seen, however, that these copies were inevitably going to have copying errors in them. The thing to remember is this: each family has its own distinctive set of errors. A scholar who knows, for example, the errors of the Byzantine family can quickly tell whether a newly discovered manuscript belongs to that family. In fact, he will sometimes know the name of the scribe who introduced a certain error into the family!

Scholars know a lot about the history of each family of manuscripts, and they keep that in mind when judging which ones to use for translating. Manuscripts that prove to be full of errors will get only a passing glance during translating; but they heavily rely on manuscripts that consistently show a dependability for accuracy. Not only is this true for individual manuscripts, it goes in a general way for the families themselves. For example, we know some of the history and the dates of the Byzantine family (the one that the KJV uses exclusively). Unfortunately these manuscripts have obvious problems in them and are dated much later than the other families, so they aren't as dependable as the others. On the other hand, the Alexandrian and Roman families are older and have proved to be more accurate — there are less errors in the texts.

And there is one more thing to consider. Scholars will often use an early *translation* of the Bible as a clue for how *their* original must have read. This is a case of detective work, and can produce some solid results. For example, they can look at a Syriac translation made in 600 AD and, reasoning backwards, figure out what the translator's Hebrew and Greek originals must have read like. Sometimes they come up with different readings than *our* existing manuscripts which date much later — therefore ours probably have an error. But the scholar must also keep in mind the *family* of originals that the Syriac translator would have been using! The translator would not have known about that family's distinctive set of errors, and they naturally would have ended up in his Syriac translation. All this is to show how complicated the business of translating and manuscript research can be.

Translations

To "translate" something means to say something in another language. You can translate a word, a phrase, or an entire book. In the case of the Bible, we are dealing with three **original** languages and one **target** language. The Old Testament was written in Hebrew and Aramaic, and the New Testament was written in Greek. The target language, in our case, is English.

Why do we translate the Bible? The main reason is that we aren't familiar with the original languages. Nobody in the Church speaks Biblical Hebrew or Aramaic or Greek anymore. If someone would give us a Bible using these languages, it would do most of us no good at all — we wouldn't understand them. The only people who can understand these languages well enough to speak them are a few scholars. Even seminary students learn only enough of the languages to stumble, at best, through the text with the constant help of dictionaries and grammars!

The problem is that we *must* have the Bible. Just because it is written in ancient languages doesn't mean that we can forget about it. So the Church's job now, before we can even begin to study the Bible, is to get it into our language so that we can understand the words.

There are two ways to translate something. The first way is **literally**, which means that you find an exact equivalent in English for every Greek and Hebrew word in the original. For example, here is John 1:1 —

Ἐν   ἀρχῇ   ἦν   ὁ   λόγος

In [*the*] beginning was the Word

For each Greek word there is an exact English word. (The first "the" in square brackets is to show that it was added in English to make a smoother translation; it isn't in the original Greek phrase.) When things are this simple, translation is an easy business. The translator only has to find the English word that best conveys the meaning of the original word.

But things aren't always this easy. Every language also has special ways of saying things that don't match the literal meaning of the words used. These are called *idioms*, and we are always using them. For example, if I say that I'm going to "run down to the store," this is an idiom — I *don't* mean what the words literally say. I'm not going to "run" (I will probably drive there!) and the store may not be "down" from where I am now. But there's nothing wrong with saying it like this; it's just that we use words in special ways to achieve a *new meaning* that the original words don't mean by themselves.

Greek and Hebrew, as you would expect, are full of idioms; so we have to translate the Bible **idiomatically** as well as literally. That makes the job of translating much more difficult. For example, here is a verse that we must translate idiomatically in order to make sense of it:

$$\text{Τί} \quad \text{ἐμοί καί σοί γύναι;}$$

What   to me   and   to you,   woman?

This is what Jesus said (literally!) to his mother at the wedding at Cana (John 2:4). It sounds so harsh to our English ears that *no* version will translate it literally. They *all* choose to translate it idiomatically, because they know that it has a meaning that you can't see by looking only at the literal words used. Here is how three different translations handle the idiom:

Dear woman, why do you involve me? (NIV)
Woman, what have I to do with thee? (KJV)
You must not tell me what to do. (TEV)

The point is that English also has a *peculiar way* (or idiom) of saying the same idea that best conveys what the Biblical writer *meant*, not necessarily what the separate words are. He wrote the way that people naturally spoke in those days; the burden is on the translator to learn how to translate their expressions accurately in order to help us know their true meaning.

A faithful translation will accurately report not only the literal words used, but the idioms used as well. This means that, when you compare the translation with the original, you will occasionally find places where the English doesn't match the Greek or Hebrew word for word; the translator chose *our* way of saying what the original phrase meant, not what it literally says. This is because the translator knew that the original phrase was an idiom and wasn't meant to be understood literally. So, rather than being disturbed at the translator for "taking liberties with the text," we should appreciate his deeper insight into the language as he shows us what the writer was *really* saying.

Of course one can go wrong in either direction when translating. Ignoring the idioms and translating everything literally is a superficial way of doing the job; in fact, some of the things you will come up with will be ridiculous! No language translates literally a hundred percent into another language. For one thing, the customs and cultures are different enough to cause different ways of expressing oneself. On the other hand, a translation that insists on turning everything into idioms is not being honest with the text. We know from our own language that we usually mean exactly what we say; not everything we say is an idiom. The point, then, is that the translator has to be good at his work. He must be determined to be honest with the text and treat every single word with great respect. Idiomatic translation is only allowed when the original meant it to be that way, and then it must be used to convey the true meaning.

The Bible has always been translated into other languages. The Israelites didn't always speak Hebrew. When they began to mix freely with other nations, they found it more convenient to speak the language of business — Aramaic — and soon they dropped speaking Hebrew even among themselves. This started about 700 BC. Hebrew became then, as it is now, the language of the scholars. By Jesus' time, for example, the common man spoke Aramaic instead of the language of the Scriptures. In order to accommodate the people, therefore, the Old Testament was first translated into Aramaic.

Some Jews moved to other parts of the world and of course dropped their mother tongue in favor of their adopted country. In that time the language of the empire (outside of Mesopotamia) was Greek. So from 300-200 BC the Jews translated their Scriptures into Greek; this is the Bible we call the *Septuagint*. It was of uneven quality — different scholars worked on different books of the Bible, and some did a better job than others — but it served the purpose and quickly became *the* Bible for Jews around the civilized world. This was the translation, by the way, that Paul and the other apostles used as they wrote and preached the Gospel. When they quoted from the Scriptures, it was the Greek Septuagint that they quoted from, not the original Hebrew Bible.

Other early translations were Arabic, Coptic, Ethiopic, Persian, Syriac, Latin — in fact, the Bible was translated into the language of many countries where the Jews and Christians went to live. The Latin translation, by the way, is commonly called the *Vulgate* and was done by the famous scholar Jerome in 400 AD.

In more modern times the same problem exists. Christians don't usually know Greek or Hebrew, so they need the Bible translated into their own tongue before they can understand it. One of the most famous translations was Martin Luther's German Bible, which is still used by German speaking people because it was so well done. Famous English translations were the Tyndale Bible, Wycliffe's translation, the King James Version, the American Standard Version, the Revised Standard Version, and the New International Version. At present, the Bible has been translated into over 1000 languages used by people around the world.

All these translations are for the purpose of getting the Word of God from the original languages into the language that people use, so that they can know the truth about God.

Can we trust the Bible?

So, can we still trust the Bible, now that we know some of its history? Let's review the facts:

- *First*, God in his Providence has preserved the Bible in a miraculous way through the ages. Unlike other books in history, the Bible has maintained its message and basic purity in spite of accidents, carelessness, and maliciousness on the part of man. The Bible we have now is almost identical to the Bible that the Early Church had, as well as the Scriptures of the Israelites.

- *Second*, the differences in manuscripts are over trivia in spelling and minor words. Nothing in the way of doctrine or truth that we need for our faith has changed in the least.

- *Third*, what God does is perfect; man introduces imperfections when he works with it. It's just like the Church, which is the body of Christ: man's errors and outright sins against it doesn't touch the vitality and reality of the Church; it still lives and grows by God's power. The Bible still tells us the truth in spite of man's interference with it. Fortunately the problems are small, and dedicated researchers can minimize man's additions to allow us to see God's Word as God originally intended it.

In light of all this, it's really dishonest that people have rejected the Bible because of its "problems." It is still God's Word in its fullest sense, and we will be saved by it – or judged by it – at the end of time. We have no other written source of God's truth.

Geography and Culture

The history of the Bible takes place in the Middle East. The Old Testament in particular focuses on Israel, with the beginning stories (of Creation and the call of Abraham) starting in the region of present day Iran and Iraq. Genesis ends up, and Exodus begins, in Egypt. But except for the mention of a few other nations around Israel throughout the histories, Canaan is the center of the story.

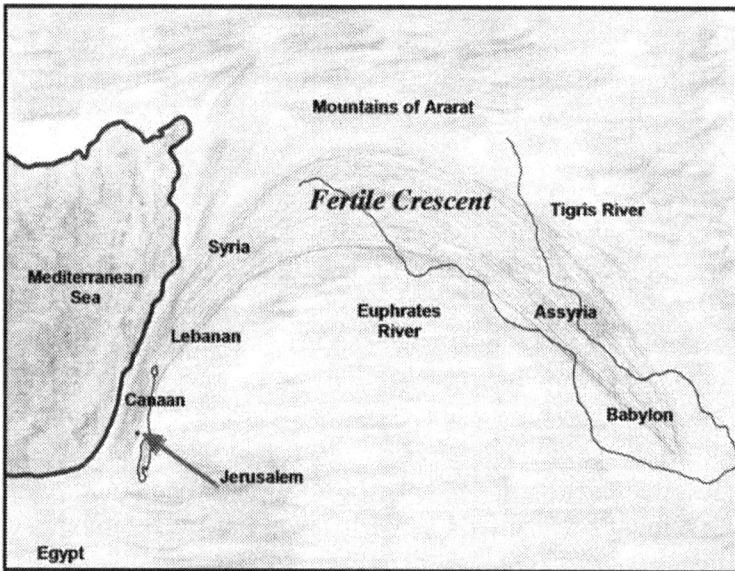

Figure 3 – The Middle East

As you can see from the map in **Figure 3**, there is a natural arc in how the rivers and coastline swing from the lower right of the map (where Ur is, present day Kuwait) up the Euphrates and Tigris Rivers, through Syria, down along the coast through Lebanon and past Jerusalem, and finally down into Egypt. This arc is called the *Fertile Crescent*, because it's the only place where there is abundant vegetation in that area! Everything else outside the arc is dry desert or mountains and unfit for settled habitation.

That means that Israel was right in the middle of things. Trade caravans followed the Fertile Crescent back and forth from Babylon to Egypt. And with traders also came the military of many countries, looking for conquests. So that meant that Israel was open to attack from all directions! This explains why so many of the kings of Israel after Solomon's day were eager to make treaties with their stronger neighbors; they had almost no natural protection from their enemies, so it made sense (to them, anyway!) to try the political solution.

Canaan is a land of mountains and plains. The Israelites first settled in the mountain region, because the Philistines were too well entrenched in the coastal area along the Mediterranean Sea. The drawing below shows the lay of the land.

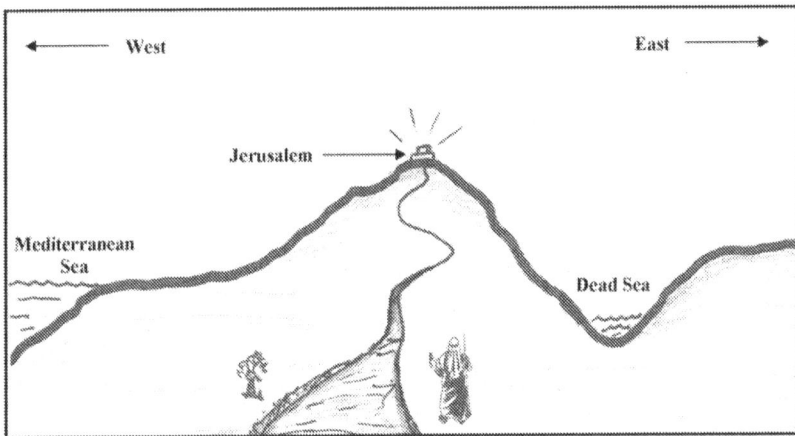

Figure 4 – Cross-section of Palestine – the man is
in Beersheba pointing north toward Jerusalem

In **Figure 4**, you see a cross-section of the land of Israel – from west to east, and you're looking at it from the south – toward the north (the drawing is *not* to scale!). To the left, along the Mediterranean Sea, is the coastal area where the Philistines lived. Notice that the mountain range runs like a spine from south to north through Canaan. Jerusalem sits along the top of the ridge. To the right of Jerusalem the mountains fall off to the Jordan River valley, then rises to a high plateau that extends off to the right into the desert. The Israelites occupied the land from Dan in the north to Beer-Sheba in the south.

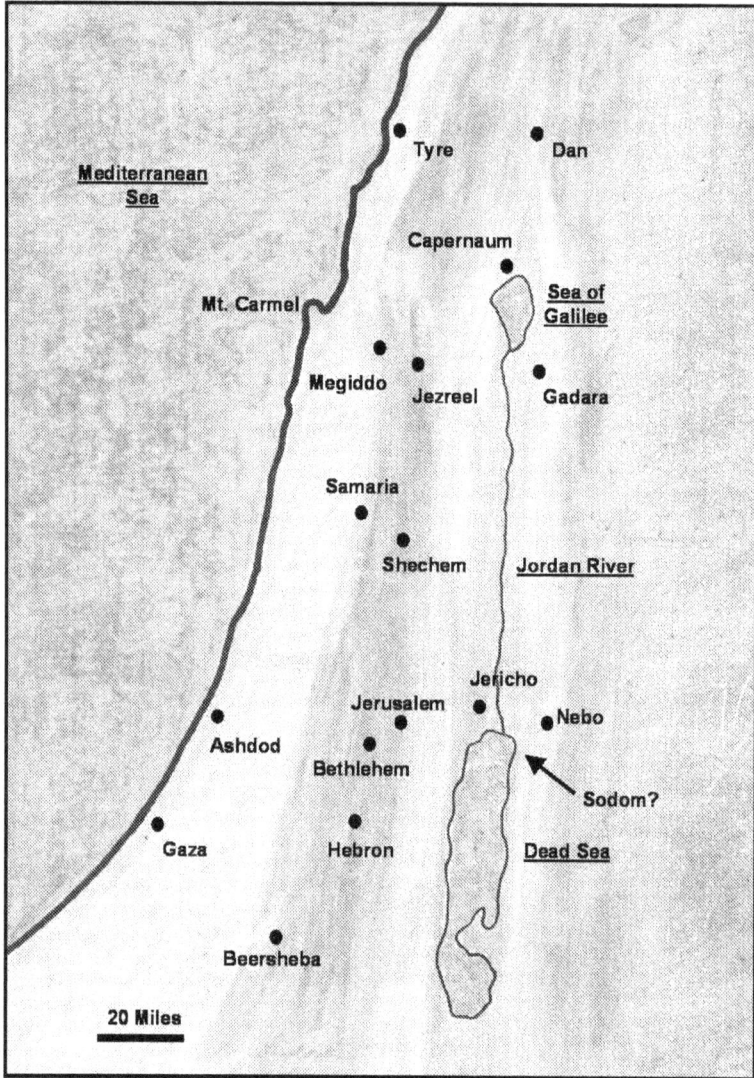

Figure 5 – Palestine

The story of the Bible is set in Canaan (see **Figure 5**), a strip of land on the eastern shore of the Mediterranean Sea. (For more detailed maps of Palestine, please consult those in the back of your Bible – most editions of the Bible will have excellent maps showing the geography of Israel, and the itinerate ministries of Christ and Paul.) The land itself isn't very big – about 130 miles north to south, 35 miles across the top from west to east, and 90 miles across the bottom. On the larger scale it sits on the western edge of what is called the Middle East, a large area of land that was home to some of the world's most powerful empires in history. As a matter of fact, aside from the history of the Jews and the ministry of Christ and the apostles, Canaan was a small pawn in the never-ending shuffle of power between such kingdoms as Assyria, Egypt, Babylon, Persia, Syria, Turkey, and modern day Iran and Iraq.

Being a coastal country, Canaan naturally changes in geography as it moves away from the Mediterranean toward the desert behind it. It has four types of land area, each type running north and south like long strips through Canaan: *first*, the flat coastal plain on the edge of the sea; *second*, the abruptly rising mountains; *third*, the mountains fall off sharply into the trough where the Jordan River runs from the Sea of Galilee down to the Dead Sea; *fourth*, a plain rises out of that trough and extends into the desert.

Rainfall varies widely over Canaan. Most of the rain falls in the northern part of the land, mostly around Dan and Mt. Hermon in the north and gradually tapering off as you move south to Jerusalem. By the time you get to Beersheba in the far south there is very little rain during the year. Almost all of the rain falls in the winter months, from December to February. The rest of the year is usually exceptionally dry and very hot.

Over thousands of years the amount of forestation in Canaan has dramatically changed. There used to be thick forests covering the mountains of Israel. Man's inexhaustible needs for wood and grazing land took a heavy toll on Israel's greenery. Because of the need for wood for housing and heating and shipping and iron smelting, and clearing out pastures for herds and areas for towns, and the inevitable erosion that took over, the land today is in very different shape than it was 1000-2000 years before Christ.

Canaan was a natural crossroads for the Middle East. Because travelers didn't want to risk the dangers of desert journeys, they moved through Palestine on their way south to Egypt or north and east to

Mesopotamia. There were well-traveled roads that ran the length of Israel, both along the shore of the Mediterranean and along the mountain ridge from Dan to Beersheba. Merchants and armies and kings and slavers all traveled these roads – which means that the Jews had a wonderful view of how the rest of the world lived. They heard all the gossip from distant lands, they saw the customs of other peoples, they bought and sold to these travelers, and – more importantly – they were constantly in danger of being attacked by traveling bands or armies. It was just too easy, without natural defenses, for a powerful neighbor to march in along the roads and lay siege to Israelite towns and cities. Enemies could pick them off like shooting fish in a barrel.

On a map you will notice the two cities Megiddo and Jezreel. They lie in a trough between a triangle of mountain ranges – Mt. Carmel to the west, the range on the south that extends down to Jerusalem, and the range on the north reaching up from Dan to Turkey. That trough is a valley that lies at the crossing of roads going north, south and east – the perfect place for a meeting of armies. As a matter of fact, it was the site of some terrible battles between Israel and other nations, and the Scriptures use this place as the picture of the final battle between nations at the end of time – Armageddon, the "mountain (the Hebrew word for mountain is *har*, which loses its initial "h" when it moves into English) of Megiddo."

There was a main road that branched east, away from the north-south road that runs alongside the Mediterranean Sea. It crossed the mountains in the area of Jerusalem and Bethlehem, plunged down into the Jordan River valley, and then turned and ran north along the river past the Sea of Galilee and up into northern Mesopotamia. It was on this road, the place where it leaves the high mountains east of Jerusalem and overlooks the Jordan River below, that the Good Samaritan found a Jew lying helplessly on the road – a victim of the ever-present robbers that hid among the rocks and crags along the roads in those days.

The Dead Sea is the lowest spot on earth. It lies in the southern part of the Jordan River valley. One can look down from the edge of the mountains just ten miles east of Jerusalem and see over much of that lower valley – the Jordan River running into the Dead Sea and the northern section of the Sea. In fact, scholars think that Sodom and Gomorrah, long thought to lie on the southern edge of the Dead Sea, actually were on the northern edge; their reasoning is that the Bible states that:

> Early the next morning Abraham got up and returned to the place where he had stood before the Lord. He looked down toward Sodom and Gomorrah, toward all the land of the plain, and he saw dense smoke rising from the land, like smoke from a furnace. (Genesis 19:27-28)

Jerusalem lies along the top of the central mountain range of Israel, nestled among some peaks that provided a natural barrier against enemies. One peak formed part of the city itself – Mt. Zion. As you read some of the Psalms you will notice that they are called "songs of ascent" – this is literally true. Jews came from all over Israel to worship at the Temple in Jerusalem at proscribed feasts, and as they came close to the city they had to climb *up* to the city in the mountains, and especially up to the Temple on Mt. Zion in the middle of the city. As they traveled up to Jerusalem on festival occasions they sang these songs in anticipation of the worship ceremony on the Temple Mount.

Culture

Even within the pages of the Bible itself there were widely different customs that the different peoples of those days practiced. Without getting into the more obvious details – clothing, food, weapons, means of travel, shelter, etc. – we will look at some of the broader elements of their culture that explain much of what we may find puzzling in the stories of the New Testament.

One of the biggest differences between their world and ours was the way the local community operated. We are individuals at heart; it doesn't really matter to us what the rest of the community does as long as it doesn't interfere with what *we* want to do. We are willing to help out in some community matters – we raise money for a new fire truck or mow an elderly person's yard for them – but then we retreat to the shelter of our own homes where nobody can interfere with us.

But the culture of the Middle East was centered on the local community. The good of the group took precedence over the good of the individual. This was out of sheer necessity, because those were the days when there was no local police force to handle social problems; the men of a town had to decide what was good for everyone, and then everyone was expected to follow their instructions or people would inevitably die. Such basic necessities that we take for granted, like water and food, were community resources that everyone had to work for and share if all would have enough. Their work was for each other: instead of our way of traveling 10-20 miles to a factory or office where we do impersonal work to accomplish things that benefit people we will probably never meet, those people shoed each other's horses and built each other's furniture and traded milk and meat with each other in order to make a living. In other words, everyone's destiny depended on each other; each man's life could succeed only if the community itself succeeded.

So there were many times when the desires of the individual had to take second place to the desires of the community, simply because rugged individualism was not only unwise but it was dangerous to the good of the whole. We stand aghast at the law in the Old Testament which said that parents of a rebellious son had to bring him to the community leaders and themselves throw the first stones at him to kill him. (Deuteronomy 21:18-21) How could the Law expect parents to treat their son like this, even if he *were* rebellious? But considered in the context of the community there was no other safe recourse for everyone involved. A man who proved to be rebellious to his parents was only going to cause trouble for the whole town, and they didn't need that. He just may be the downfall of the town! At the very least he wouldn't carry his share of the load of work and responsibility, which meant that everyone else had to work extra hard to make up for his laziness or destructive habits. That would be like having an enemy within the ranks; many a town had fallen to the rape and slaughter and destruction of alien armies because of one man's sin. So rather than saddling the community with a problem like that and causing everyone pain and trouble, the parents were expected to themselves deal with the problem before it got to that stage. Their individual needs were second in importance to the needs of the community. Besides, by letting him live they were only postponing the inevitable (if it was inevitable – I'm sure that *every* "rebellious son" was not put to death, simply because we *all* have sin in our hearts! This was only for hard-core cases, such as we have in our society); the community would later find it necessary to put him to death for worse crimes if he were allowed to live, and then the shame would never leave his parents' household.

The community's success meant success for the individual. If there was plenty of rain, and the bugs and birds didn't eat all of the harvest, the whole town benefited from the harvest; then the people would celebrate together with festivals. But if danger or famine struck the town, everyone suffered; there was no such thing as insurance in those days, and one family couldn't go out on their own to avoid the hazards of the community – it was do or die for all of the people together. If life was good, they all enjoyed it; if life was bad, they died together.

The family itself was also different from our modern family, and the reason was again because of survival and efficiency. We are individualists to the core, and usually we don't think twice about making the family serve our own personal purposes. But with them it was the other way around; each member served the purposes of the family. They put aside any thoughts of doing things that they wanted if it didn't fit in with the family's immediate needs.

In the first place, "family" was usually much larger than Mom and Dad and brother and sister. It wasn't unusual for uncles and aunts and grandparents and cousins to share a house together – the family was actually a small community in itself! They had to do it this way because life was rough, and trying to make it on your own meant certain failure. One needs lots of labor to manage flocks of sheep or cattle; one needs many hands to harvest a field of grain when the only tools were sickle and fork! Gathering and storing and preparing food, and making clothing, were jobs that lasted the year round; and that took up all the time available from sun-up to sundown, since they lacked the fast efficiency of modern technology that we have today. So it made much more sense to stick together rather than to separate, and newlyweds would take their place in their parents' homes and farms rather than go off by themselves to pursue their own "careers."

In the family, Dad was boss. He had that right in the eyes of the community, and he also had the responsibility that went with the job. He plowed the fields, he tended the herds, he attended community meetings and shouldered his share of the community work. When it came time to defend the town against their enemies, he took sword in hand and risked his life for his family. The average life expectancy of men in those days wasn't very long, given their hard labor and high death rate in battle. So nobody questioned his authority; in fact, respect for Father ran much deeper in that society than it does in ours. We think nothing of doing our own thing even if it runs against the wishes of our parents; they wouldn't have dared to think that way. The father had years of experience that the children needed if they hoped to make it in life as well as he had. If they got on his good side, they were assured of his inheritance and therefore of a secure future. And he bought the right – with his hard labor and protection and respect from his peers in the community – to be held in honor by his children. A man who had rebellious and self-willed children hid his head in shame when he went about the town.

Women never strayed from the home by themselves; not only was it not safe, but there was nothing in town for them to do like there is in our society. A woman who wandered the streets alone on her own business was considered a prostitute, because there wasn't any other reason she would be out there unless it was on family business. Women had plenty to do at home without wandering around doing their own thing: preparing meals (which took up a large part of the day), taking care of the children, carrying water (a small detail to us but a major chore in those days), planting and hoeing fields, making and mending clothing (again a long, involved process with the primitive tools that they had). If the women didn't pull their weight in this way, the family would literally starve or go in rags!

Children were extremely important in those days. In our own time children seem to be more of a nuisance than a blessing; they get in the way of our careers or whatever we want to enjoy in life. To many in our day, children are a curse! But to the Israelites, children were a blessing from God: it meant ready hands (if not willing!) in the fields and family business. They also served as a retirement plan: when the parents were too old to carry on, the children took over the family business and cared for Mom and Pop as long as they lived. That seems unfair to us that the children would be so bound by their family ties like this. But the day was coming when those children would need the same help from *their* children – the system worked. Nobody minded when everyone benefited.

A word about work in those days. Unless one was rich (and there were very few who were) one could expect to work as long as there was daylight. That meant that there was almost no time for leisure or hobbies or taking it easy. In our culture we think ourselves ill-used if we work more than eight hours a day. In their day, they felt that they had a chance to survive – and therefore were blessed by God – if they had strength and health to work for 14-18 hours a day. There was no such thing as a vacation for them. They worked all their lives, and usually had only a place to live, a field to plow, perhaps some pasture land, maybe some flocks of sheep, to show for their hard work when they died. One's inheritance in those days would have made us laugh at its pitiful scarcity; but it meant the success of the children if they used it as wisely as their parents did.

The military life of those ancient people was also much different than we experience in our culture. Because of the necessity placed on them by their circumstances, nobody was exempt from service unless they were physically unable to take sword in hand. Young and old helped to defend the town from attackers; nobody argued about such matters when the town was liable to be burned to the ground and all the men and children inside murdered and the women carried off to grace the beds of their enemies! It was a hard world, and they did whatever was necessary to protect themselves and their families. And there were many times when the men were called out to travel across country to help other towns against their enemies. They did it willingly for a couple of reasons: first, those enemies, if successful against one town, would probably be at their own doorstep someday; and second, their community spirit extended to the whole race, and they were willing to die to help the entire Jewish nation succeed. The good of the nation outweighed the good of the local town and the individual.

Social agreements were fascinating in those days. Remember that they had no police force. When two men made an agreement with each other, they were expected to make sure *themselves* that the other man kept to the agreement. If one reneged on the deal, the other man had the right, in the community's eyes, to take whatever action that would be necessary to get what was due him. Who else would do it for him? The community would support him in his struggle for justice, but it was up to him to get it; nobody else could do it for him. So if he was cheated and had no way to force the other man to make it right, he was just cheated, that's all. That's why there was a strange-sounding law in the Old Testament about accidental killings: if a man accidentally killed another, the victim's family had the right to pursue the killer and kill him – unless he found safety in a City of Refuge and convinced the elders of that town that he was really innocent. Otherwise the victim's family had the right to his life. And if they didn't kill him, nobody else would; it was *their* responsibility to take care of the matter because nobody else had the right to his life.

Greek influence

Since coming back from the Exile in Babylon the Jews were rarely left alone by other nations. For a time they came under Greek influence (from the conquering armies of Alexander the Great), and it showed in their culture. Many Jews absolutely refused to have anything to do with the foreigners; but some Jews, looking for new experiences and contacts (perhaps profitable ones!) with the outside world, took on Greek ways and dress. This was always a bone of contention in Jewish circles: there were those who were "liberal" and trained their children in the ways of the "world," and there were conservatives who fought to resist outside influences, and raised their children to be faithful, orthodox Jews.

One influence, as we've seen already, that laid a foundation for the future of the Church was the fact that the Greek language became part of everyday life. Even when the Romans conquered the area later, most people in Palestine knew Greek and communicated on paper with that language. The apostles all wrote their letters in Greek because their churches, that were found all over the Roman empire, all knew and spoke Greek fluently.

But Greek influence went deeper than just the language. Philo, for example, who was a Jewish philosopher, was as Greek in his thinking as he could be. He wrote a great deal about the "mysteries" of the universe, and even wrote about the Logos – the mystical principle of the Word of God that lay as a foundation underneath God's Creation. His teaching no doubt influenced the apostle John as he too wrote about the Logos – the Word that was with God in the beginning, through whom all things were created. (John 1:1-5)

Roman influence

The Romans, as we've seen, conquered Palestine also as they made their sweep around the Mediterranean. The country was carved up into sections, and the family of the Herods ruled during the time of Jesus and the Apostles.

The Roman government imposed several things on the Jews: *first*, they stationed garrisons of soldiers all through the land to keep the peace and enforce the laws. *Second*, they had their own governor there in Jerusalem to rule over the land in Caesar's name. *Third*, they imposed taxes on the country, and used local Jewish officials to collect them and send them on to Rome.

Aside from this overwhelming political control, the Romans actually affected the Jewish state very little in the way of culture. The main outside cultural influence that the Jews had to contend with was the Greek culture.

Rabbinical influence

After the Exile to Babylon, the Jews were extremely sensitive about the Law. The reason they were punished in the first place was because they weren't taking certain laws seriously. So in order to avoid further displeasure from the Judge of the earth, they resolved to do whatever they could to fulfill the Law as best they could.

After Ezra returned to Jerusalem we begin to see the great teachers of the Law that culminated in the rabbis of the New Testament. Soon after Ezra's time, the Oral Law was created – a commentary and extension of the Mosaic Law that explored further how to carry out the

Law of God in every imaginable circumstance in life. For a long time this Oral Law existed side by side with the written Mosaic Law – a rabbi, or teacher of the Law of God, would learn both systems.

In Jesus' day the Oral Law had reached epic proportions. They had devised thousands of case-law studies on how to please God in every aspect of life. For example, the Jews tried to list every form of work that might be prohibited by the Fourth Commandment –

> Remember the Sabbath day by keeping it holy. Six days you shall labor and do all your work, but the seventh day is a Sabbath to the LORD your God. On it you shall not do any work, neither you, nor your so or daughter, nor your manservant or maidservant, nor your animals, nor the alien within your gates. (Exodus 20:8-10)

They figured out, for instance, that paring your fingernails is work and therefore illegal to do on the Sabbath!

There were three main "parties" of Jews, so to speak, in Jesus' day. The **Pharisees** were the best known; they were the legal experts and the keepers of the Oral Law. They also believed in the resurrection of the dead and a future life. Jesus most often had religious arguments with the Pharisees. The **Sadducees** were less interested in the moral aspects of Judaism, certainly not interested in the world to come (they didn't believe in it!), and very interested in national and local politics. And the **Essenes** were a fringe group that believed in the coming of the Messiah. They mainly gathered in desert communities to separate themselves from the world and prepare themselves morally for the last days.

The Jews had a sensitive relationship with the Romans. Though the Romans maintained ultimate power in Palestine, they let the Jews keep their own ruling body to decide religious, moral, and some political issues. This body of elders was called the Sanhedrin and consisted usually of 70 leaders from around the nation. They were not allowed to put anybody to death – a capital offense was a crime against the state, and therefore came under Roman jurisdiction. Thus they themselves could find Jesus guilty, but they then had to convince the Romans that he had done something against the state – and therefore against Caesar – in order to have him executed.

The third Temple, built by Herod, was still the center of Jewish life. It was a massive structure and one of the marvels of the ancient world. And during the religious festivals, Jerusalem was a hub of multitudes who came from all over the land of Palestine as well as from Jewish communities from the civilized world. But the Jews also had the **synagogue**: a local body of Jews in each community who gathered weekly to read the Scripture and discuss points of Jewish law. It corresponded somewhat to the idea of the local Christian church, and exerted a tremendous influence in Judaism not only in Biblical days but throughout history into our time.

Probably the one apostle that came under the influence of the rabbis the most was Paul. He was trained to be a rabbi: he was –

> Circumcised on the eighth day, of the people of Israel, of the tribe of Benjamin, a Hebrew of Hebrews; in regard to the law, a Pharisee; as for zeal, persecuting the church; as for legalistic righteousness, faultless. (Philippians 3:5-6)

And you can see that rigorous legal training in how he presents his theological arguments in his letters. But it's a rabbinical training that has been baptized by the Holy Spirit. He isn't arguing for petty legalistic issues anymore, but for the mystery of the Gospel in Christ.

A Note on Archaeology

Archaeology is the study of "old things" – the remains of ancient civilizations. It's astonishing how much human history has gone before us; recorded history extends back to around 6000 BC, so for six millenia before Christ there have been generations of people – hundreds of millions of people – living and dying that we know hardly anything about. Archaeologists like to dig in the dirt and rocks for any clue of how those people lived in those days.

Biblical archaeology deals with the remains of the ancient world that might shed some light on events recorded in the Bible. Biblical archaeologists have dug up cities in Canaan (and surrounding countries) and analyzed the pottery, jewelry, weapons, buildings, writings and other artifacts to try to answer several questions:

- Can these items help fix the dates of the events recorded in the Bible?

- Can we find proof outside the Bible (in other words, in things left behind from those ancient cultures) of the existence of the people and events recorded in the Bible?

Concerning the dating problem, using only the Bible can be a little difficult to nail down actual dates of events. For example, the Exodus from Egypt occurred, according to scholars, anywhere between 1445 BC and 1250 BC, depending on how you interpret the word "generations," and how you date the length of time the Israelites stayed in Egypt under slavery. By using archaeology and the study of the surrounding cultures in that day, you may be able to narrow down the possible dates – a conservative estimate seems to lean toward the earlier date now.

But when it comes to "proving" the Bible, archaeology falls short. Unfortunately many archaeologists put too much stock in their trade and make claims that are unfounded.

First, the most that archaeology can do is tell us more about what life was like in Bible times. The Bible already does a fair job of that – we know already that people rode on donkeys and camels, wore sandals, drank wine out of skins, fought with arrows and spears and shields, made clay pots for storage, and so on. A great deal of ancient culture is revealed for us in the pages of the Bible. But it helps to widen the picture out and see the Bible as a piece in the overall ancient world; it wasn't so unique culturally from its neighbors.

Second, the Bible is not a cultural message – it is God's Word to all generations and cultures. They may have lived everyday lives like their neighbors, but their religion set them totally apart from their neighbors. It was the first instance of the Word of God shaping and transforming a culture. The point is that the Word of God continues to confront and transform cultures throughout history – including ours. So the message of the Bible is ageless; it is completely relevant to any people and culture.

What this means then is that archaeology (along with other human sciences) can't prove that the Bible was simply a product of its own time. That's exactly what many archaeologists try to do. By showing, for example, that Moses got his "Ten Commandments" from old Egyptian law-books, and the Name Yahweh actually came from one of the Egyptian gods, they think therefore that the Bible is plagiarism at the worst, and religious syncretism at best – instead of a direct revelation from God. It's usually the Liberals who are playing this game. What they want to prove is that people made the Bible up, to suit their own needs and times, using the ideas of their own culture to teach about God. But that's not the

Bible's own testimony of itself. "Thus says the Lord," and "write these words down and give them to the people" fill its pages. So, whatever we might learn through archaeology, it can't contradict the foundation of the Bible being *God's Word to man;* it's not man's word about God. [1]

In other words, when archaeologists are up to no good, they are actually trying to disprove the Word of God; when they're behaving themselves, they "discover" only that the Bible was right all along.

Third, archaeology does nothing for our faith. It doesn't really matter exactly when the Exodus occurred, or which body of water they crossed to escape Egypt, or whether anybody can find chariots in the bottom of the sea to prove the event. The text says simply that God brought his people out of Egypt, separated the water so that they could walk through unharmed, and brought the water back upon the Egyptian soldiers and drowned them all. **Faith believes the story**. The "real life" world of science can never talk us out of the awe we feel before a miracle-working God.

If you believe God's Word, you won't need a scientist to confirm it for you. We go by what God says; we may or may not accept what man says regarding the event. If the events in the Bible required scientific proof before we could believe them, then only scientists would be believers! On the contrary, the stories of the Bible are there for the simplest believers, even children, those who have no expertise in worldly matters. The truth of the Bible, as Jesus pointed out, is wide open like a door to

---

[1] And as far as culture shaping the message, the Bible never does teach that one has to wear sandals to believe in God, if you know what I mean. No culture is a prerequisite for faith; anybody can come to God and know him and please him with their lives. However, if the Bible tells us to do something specific, you can count on it that the act required is not a cultural matter – we *all* have to do it.

God's faithful people; it is shut tight against the "wisdom" of the world that needs more than God's Word to believe in him.

Probably the strongest area in archaeology that is helpful for Biblical studies is the issue of ancient Bible manuscripts. We discussed this subject a little bit already. Certainly the Dead Sea Scrolls and Tischendorff's discovery of ancient Codices of the Bible have helped translators tremendously who are trying to piece together what the original Bible must have read like. But even here, the discoveries have fallen short of making the Bible a totally new book. The differences between ancient manuscripts and even more ancient manuscripts are trivial at best – nowhere do we find any doctrinal changes, or changes in history, or anything that would alter the foundation of our faith. What the Church has believed about God and Christ (when their faith was based on the Word of God), we continue to believe in – archaeology hasn't given us any reason to put *that* God aside.

A note on archaeology

Understanding the whole Bible

The Revelation of God

It's getting harder and harder to distinguish the true from the false church. A hundred years ago the Liberals were ripping up the Bible, destroying the foundations of our historic Christian faith, and still claiming to be Christians. That brought no end of confusion to the church scene, since good people continued to attend their churches in faithful devotion while listening to the poison concocted in unbelieving seminaries and Bible schools. The entire Liberal movement pretty much emptied the Bible of its meaning and content for the average churchgoer. Sermons moved from the Bible to the social scene; authors wrote books not on Bible studies per se but on social issues and current events. Ignorance of what the Bible actually teaches was widespread. Only a few churches here and there held on tenaciously to a high view of the Bible and the importance of studying it.

Now even the conservative and evangelical Church is experiencing confusion over how it handles the Bible. Churches claim to "lift up the name of Jesus" in their ministries, and proclaim that they are "Christ-centered" in their emphasis. They say that they are Biblically-based churches, they are "Bible believing" churches. Christians looking for real answers to life respond to the advertising hype and go to these churches with high hopes, but they find the same tired themes in most of them – shallow sermons, social and political themes, psychological counseling, ignorance about large parts of the Bible, prayer meetings without power. It doesn't pay any more to put much stock in the claims of being "Christ-centered" and "Biblically based" – so many ministries claim this, it's too easy to say, and it too often turns out to be not true.

And we know we're in trouble when churches are proud about being "New Testament churches." Who authorized them to throw away three-fourths of their Bibles?! I don't remember reading anything in the Bible about God telling them to treat his Word so casually, so disrespectfully. What they're doing is disposing of 1500 years of preparatory work that God did to save his people, as if it's of no concern to them. The Jews also despised the Old Testament lessons when they rejected the ministry of Christ – because *he* was the culmination of all the Old Testament history and doctrine!

The signs are plain to see: we modern Christians obviously don't know what we are saying with the phrases "Christ-centered" and "Biblically based" when it's so easy for a ministry to claim these and then not produce a deep understanding of the whole Bible.

A man-centered religion

The Liberals claim the name Christian but they don't have the doctrine to back up that claim. If someone doesn't believe large parts of the Bible as it stands (without doctoring it up with modern culture, psychology, social issues, genetics, etc.!) then they should not call themselves "Christian." They are free to start a new religion of their own if they want, but it's not valid to claim to be Christians if they don't believe the historic doctrines of Christianity. It makes the rest of us look bad in the eyes of an unbelieving world.

The conservatives, however, need to work on giving some substance to their often-empty claims. If they want to "lift up the name of Jesus" then they ought to start teaching about Jesus! Instead, they have fallen back to name-dropping – they liberally sprinkle their lessons and sermons with the names of Christ (and God) without actually telling us much about Christ himself.

This is probably due to the fact that most of these leaders haven't been taught enough about Christ to talk about him at length. Furthermore, they weren't taught how to look for God in the Bible; they weren't trained in how to handle the Book in the way that God intended. So, because they don't have much to say about God himself, it's too easy to fall back on moralizing and prodding people into "Christian living."

This kind of ministry is actually a *man-centered* religion. Instead of focusing on God and his works, the focus is on man and what we are supposed to do. **There is no hope, no salvation in this form of ministry.** If all we can offer people looking for help is more effort on their part, we haven't helped them at all. We are pointing them to the wrong savior – themselves.

Here are a few characteristics of a man-centered religion.

- **Moralisms** – What I mean by this is a list of do's and don'ts that you pressure people into observing. Do this and this and this, and don't do that and that and that.

This is appealing to people on several fronts. First, it looks as if the Bible really is set up this way. Morals and ethics fill the Bible from front to back. The Ten Commandments stand guard over the whole book, and all the writers after Moses take us back to that Law and make sure we get the point. All of society understands that Western systems of morality came primarily from the Bible's teachings.

Second, we love to swing into action to solve problems. Just give us a glimmer of hope that our own efforts can make the problem go away and we will begin immediately on whatever you tell us to do.

So preachers and teachers will give people what they want by boiling down the entire Bible to a handy list of morals for them to observe. For example, we are told to –

- Have the **patience** of Job
- Have the **faith** of Abraham
- Have the **courage** of David
- Be **holy** like Jesus
- Avoid the **lusts** of the flesh like Joseph
- Be a **witness** like Paul

You have probably heard many more. In fact, most of the sermons and lessons you've heard over the years have probably been mostly along this line.

The problem is that we can't do these things. Even the people mentioned in this list (with the exception of Jesus) would testify that, in themselves, they could never do God's will on their own – only because *God* enabled them to do the impossible did they find themselves able to obey him. The secret was to get in touch with the God who has the answers. Though we *are* told to be like this, the Bible never leads us to believe that we can do it without God!

- **Psychology and counseling** – Sermon after sermon could easily be duplicated in the psychiatrist's chair. Are you lonely? Fellowship will lift your spirits. Do you have a problem getting along with your neighbor? Be a loving person – the problem between you and your neighbor will then solve itself. Do you need help sorting out your daily responsibilities? We can teach you how to be a Christian homemaker, a Christian businessman, a Christian athlete, a Christian parent – follow this advice, and life will become more pleasant and fulfilling for you.

It sounds as if preachers are simply giving counseling sessions from the pulpit. In fact, take out the occasional (and usually meaningless) references to God, and these sermons could easily be transcripts of psychologists of *any* religious faith telling their clients how to live a happier life. People are filling the mega-churches who cater to their home needs with family counseling sermons. There's nothing peculiarly Christian about the message; it could be just as well delivered by a Jewish rabbi or a Hindu swami.

On the other hand, a peculiarly Christian sermon or lesson should give great offense to a non-believing psychiatrist. It should go contrary to established counseling principles, because it leads man to a God who doesn't do things man's way but by his own way – by the Truth, by the Spirit, by miracle and by command.

• **Social issues** – Man is a political creature, and preachers get caught up in current events just like everyone else. So it's tempting to focus on what's going on in the world in one's "Bible" lesson. The justification for this is that the Bible supposedly speaks to current events and how Christians need to relate to what's happening around them.

So there are sermons on abortion, on women's rights, on the Presidential race, on wars, on gay marriage, on education, on entertainment (with specific movies or stars becoming the point of the sermon!) and on everything else going on under the sun.

It's true that the Bible does address all the issues of life. But it's not true that the Bible focuses on these issues. Our faith is not based on what we think of what is going on in the world; it is based on what we know about God. The same people who can write whole books on abortion, for example, don't know enough about the Old Testament to fill a sheet of paper! They would make great professors on human rights in secular schools, but they don't make good pastors leading people back to God. There is a time to pronounce God's edict on man's behavior and society's morals and practices; but it's also far too easy to major on *that* instead of focusing on knowing God – which is the believer's chief concern and duty. (John 17:3)

• **Lip service to God** – While people keep focusing on minor issues like this, they like to think that they are doing God a service. So they use his name in their sermons – "God" and "Jesus" and the "Spirit" – like sprinkling salt and pepper on a meal. By doing this, evidently, they think that God will approve of what they are saying. It makes it seem like it's a Christian lesson.

So often preachers and teachers of the Bible will do what I call "name-dropping." In other words, they use God's name and Christ's name all through their lessons, but they don't give any content to the words. They tell us that "We must believe in Jesus!" without stopping to tell us anything about Jesus. Notice the simple grammar of this sentence.

We	**must believe in**	**Jesus**
subject	*action*	*object*

The subject of a sentence does the action upon the object. In this case, the people listening are encouraged to do the action; *they* are the subject, the main focus of the lesson. Jesus is simply the passive receiver of all the work that we are counseled to do. If you don't believe that this is typical of modern Bible lessons, keep track sometime of the speakers you hear and note what they are telling you to do.

Dropping God's name throughout the sermon like this isn't teaching us about God. It's dishonest, really – there is a world of information about God in the Bible begging us to study it, holding out life to us – but we're ignoring almost all of it and simply using God's name to grace our counseling sessions or social analyses. We aren't really conveying any new information *about God* when we use his name like this.

For example, we are told to believe in God. We emphasize the word "believe" because that's something that we can do, or so we think. We like activity. But very few people actually ask themselves the obvious question – what exactly are we supposed to believe *about* God? What is the content of our faith? What is it that we see there in him? Or are we not concerned with God himself – only in our own activity of "believing" or having faith?

We are told to be good – to follow the Ten Commandments, to live a righteous life like Jesus did. Has no one noticed that the Jews themselves failed to keep those Ten Commandments over a 1500 year training period? Did everyone miss the fact that, if Jesus is the only Perfect Man to have lived on earth, then we *can't* live as he did?

We are told to devote ourselves to the Lord, to love him with all of our hearts. Whom do we love? What is it in him that would capture the heart and make it want to be devoted to him? Where is the motivation, the fire that warms the heart to the work, the vision of who God is that so draws the human heart out to God and to nothing else? What is it about God that would take away our dread of him, our innate hatred of his ways?

These examples show that we really aren't talking about God – we're talking about ourselves. No amount of name-dropping, however, will make our sermons and lessons "Christ-centered" or "Bible-based."

The main objection to a man-centered religion is that **there is no salvation in it**. If there is a central message about man all through the Bible, from front to back, it is this – man is in a desperate situation. He has offended God, he has ruined himself and God's creation, he is dying and spiritually dead, and unless something drastic is done he is off to an eternal state of misery as the universe's most infamous convict. Our only hope is for something from *outside* man, *outside* his world, to come in and rescue him. In light of this theme, it's really misleading to tell people that their own actions are the answer to their problems.

All the faith in the world won't get us close to God. Only Jesus does that. All the courage in the world won't help us stand against the Enemy. Only Jesus can protect us. Go ahead and try to love God and man with all of your heart; you will find that somewhere, sometime, that love of yours will fail and you will fall back to the innate hatred, animosity, lust, rebellion and general contrariness that every human being has in himself.

> The LORD saw how great man's wickedness on the earth had become, and that every inclination of the thoughts of his heart was only evil all the time. (Genesis 6:5)

> There is not a righteous man on earth who does what is right and never sins. (Ecclesiastes 7:20)

> The heart is deceitful above all things and beyond cure. Who can understand it? (Jeremiah 17:9)

> So I find this law at work: When I want to do good, evil is right there with me. For in my inner being I delight in God's Law; but I see another law at work in the members of my body, waging war against the law of my mind and making me a prisoner of the law of sin at work within my members. What a wretched man I am! Who will rescue me from this body of death? (Romans 7:21-24)

If you don't give someone hope that a Person greater than they are has the power and determination to rescue them, they will end up with no hope – especially when they keep trying to do this Christianity thing and it doesn't work out.

When Jesus came to this world, he found the Jews bound by the same man-centered religion. Instead of learning the right lesson from their history, the Jews considered themselves experts in the Law and righteous enough to please God with their own works. We call this *legalism* – because the emphasis is not on God's grace and mercy to sinners, but expecting a reward from God, and entrance into Heaven, for our good works. When Jesus offered them a way of escape from their sins by his own righteousness and his blood sacrifice to cover their sins, they rejected him completely. God's response to the Jews was to cut them off from the Vine, to take the Gospel to the Gentiles.

A shallow understanding of the Bible

This may come as a surprise to the average churchgoer, but seminaries and Bible colleges are largely at fault for the ignorance in the churches. If the Christians in the pews don't know the Bible and know almost nothing about God, it's probably because the church leaders failed to teach them. And almost always you can track this problem back to the schools who "taught" the church leaders – the teaching didn't include, ironically enough, information on the Bible's true message.

And when you look at many sermons and Bible lessons today, it's no surprise. There is hardly any real content in these lessons. Leaders may *claim* that they are Bible-based, but that doesn't make it true. They may claim that they are centered on Christ, but unless they really focus on Christ in their lesson and give content about him, the claim is baseless and misleading.

This is what is taught in seminaries and Bible colleges: beginning Bible surveys, systematic theology, church history, church management, missions, counseling, and the Biblical languages. The beginning Bible surveys are pretty much for the purpose of familiarizing the student with the characters, stories, history and background of the Bible. It does almost nothing for preparing the student for in-depth Bible studies, and certainly doesn't take them through the great themes of the Bible in a vigorous way. So, with little or no training in how to handle the Bible, the pastors and teachers who come away with this "training" are expected to stand before a congregation who will most definitely *not* be interested in church history, systematic theology, church management, missions, and the Biblical languages, and teach them. Teach them what? They weren't trained in Bible study themselves; how can they give the congregation the fruit of their labors if they don't know how to handle the text?

What makes this worse is that the Old Testament suffers the most. The standard line in seminary is that the Old Testament is a poorly developed picture of God's truth, that the New Testament is much better for understanding our faith. So if not officially then practically speaking the pastors are trained to stay away from the Old Testament – and of course that attitude filters down to the churches they minister in.

First let's take the case of the more obvious problem. It really frustrates me to hear people boast about being "New Testament Christians." That's like hearing a doctor brag about only going to the last year of medical training – the year of internship in the hospital! I wouldn't trust myself under his care. He can't possibly know what he's talking about if he doesn't do the preliminary years of studies first. In the same way, how can a pastor or teacher understand the New Testament if he doesn't study *and use* the Old Testament too? After all, the New Testament itself claims that it is the Old Testament religion raised to a spiritual level. And it also sends us back to the Old for many explanations that it doesn't have time to go over. For example, the writer of Hebrews was about to launch into a detailed study of Melchizedek – but he stops first, and tells his readers that they probably aren't ready for this. They need to go back to the Old Testament and get some of the fundamentals of the faith first before they move into deeper spiritual issues.

> We have much to say about this, but it is hard to explain because you are slow to learn. In fact, though by this time you ought to be teachers, you need someone to teach you the elementary truths of God's Word all over again. You need milk, not solid food! (Hebrews 5:11-12)

This means that "New Testament Christians" can't possibly understand how Christ is the Son of David, how he is the heir of the covenant given to Abraham, that he is the Creator who uses the methods of Creation in his ministry, that he is the fulfillment of the Mosaic Law – and on and on we could go. They can't know what he was really doing when he chose his disciples, when he worked miracles, when he lived the sinless life, when he rose from the dead and ascended to Heaven – these were all the finishing touches to the great project started and developed in the *Old* Testament. They will miss the significance of his Name (the very name of the Old Testament God), of his ways and works (first taught to the Jews, starting all the way back at the Exodus itself), and the eternal Temple he is building (according to the pattern shown to Moses on Mt. Sinai).

After we've exposed the shallowness of the "New Testament Christians," we could also apply the same charge of ignorance to those who supposedly hold the Old Testament in the same regard as the New. Do they really understand these fundamental truths? Do they realize that the Old Testament is full of Christian doctrine?

> From infancy you have known the holy Scriptures, [*which in Paul's day was the **Old** Testament!*] which are able to make you **wise for salvation through faith in Christ Jesus**. (2 Timothy 3:15)

Or do they still hold to the mistaken notion, taught extensively across most Bible schools, that the Old Testament religion is actually primitive Israelite cultic belief and practice that we Christians don't have to spend much time on? Do they actually go back to the Old Testament and use it as a textbook for Christianity, or do they hesitate to put much stock in an undeveloped system and turn rather to the "fully developed" statement of our faith in Paul's letters?

Unless you see that the Old and New form one single system – that both are indispensable to our Christian faith – then the Christianity you will teach and preach will end up to be shallow. There's just not much depth in today's preaching – as we can see when people are continually encouraged to get saved every Sunday, and Sunday School lessons invariably go back to Paul's missionary journeys, and home Bible groups just get together and share opinions and feelings, and Wednesday night "Bible studies" are nothing more than long lists of prayer requests with a brief catch-all prayer at the end. If you don't have much to say about the Bible, then of course you will look somewhere else for topics – like current events and being a Christian wife and mother and the social ills of our culture.

It's a logical yet tragic problem. The Bible is about God. So if we don't understand the Bible (to the degree that Paul describes it – the "deep truths of the faith" – 1 Timothy 3:9) then we won't understand

God.   That leaves only man to preach about – our duties, our
responsibilities, our works, our glory.

Man can be a stubborn creature sometimes. He will hang on to
what he is doing, because he believes in it, for a long time – even when
it isn't doing him any good but rather a lot of harm. I heard of one
pastor who, after years of being part of a denomination and a church
that energetically and devotedly kept saying "praise the Lord" in their
services, actually stopped and asked himself, "what am I praising the
Lord *about*?" It struck him that they had been using empty words with
no meaning. It sounded good, but it did nobody any good. Just asking
that simple question, however, turned him around to face the God he
supposedly believed in but knew little about.

God becomes the focus

A God-centered ministry, on the other hand, actually turns to God
himself and starts studying *him*.

This might seem like a strange exercise at first, but its strangeness
only proves the point. We are so used to thinking about ourselves that
we are at first confused and uneasy when we try to think about *only*
God. We feel that we've done Bible study when we see ourselves, or
something that relates to our personal situation, in the passage. The
saints in Bible times, however, were masters at studying God.

Those of you who have been married (or have thought about it!)
know exactly what I mean. When you found the one you loved, you
didn't focus on how *you* felt, or what *you* did – you focused exclusively
on how the object of your affections looked or what they did. Their
every look, their every move, fascinated you, captivated you, held you
in a helpless wonder.

It's interesting that the Bible puts our worship of God in the same
terms. Like a marriage, God becomes our Lover, our Husband, our
Provider. The Bible talks about the beauty of Christ, the faithfulness of
the Father, the majesty and glory of God on his throne. We read of his
works and the ways he does things. The more clearly we see him, the
easier it is to be fascinated with this God and fall in love with him.

Quickly we lose sight of ourselves as we fill our eyes and hearts and minds with the knowledge of God.

This is, after all, our duty. Jesus said it plainly.

> *Love* the Lord your God with all your heart and with all your soul and with all your mind. This is the first and greatest commandment. (Matthew 22:37)

Now love doesn't happen in ignorance. You can't love your wife or husband without knowing anything about them! In the same way, you will find that, until you learn a good deal about God, you are going to feel anything but love for him. Sinners don't love a holy God; rebels don't love a King; immoral wretches don't love a righteous Judge. This is, in fact, what many people will discover at the Gates of Heaven. He doesn't like them, and they're not going to like him.

> Not everyone who says to me, 'Lord, Lord,' will enter the kingdom of Heaven, but only he who does the will of my Father who is in Heaven. Many will say to me on that day, 'Lord, Lord, did we not prophesy in your name, and in your name drive out demons and perform many miracles?' Then I will tell them plainly, 'I never knew you. Away from me, you evildoers!' (Matthew 7:21-23)

Look, for example, at the Psalms. Here is a wealth of information about God. In Psalm 105 is a list of important truths about the Lord that we need to know – data that is worth our time to mine out of Scripture, like gold.

> Give thanks to the LORD, call on his Name; make known among the nations what he has done. Sing to him, sing praise to him; tell of all his wonderful acts. Glory in his holy Name; let the hearts of those who seek the LORD rejoice. Look to the LORD and his strength; seek his face always. Remember the wonders he has done, his miracles, and the judgments he pronounced, O descendants of Abraham his servant, O sons of Jacob,

his chosen ones. He is the LORD our God; his judgments are in all the earth. He remembers his covenant forever, the word he commanded, for a thousand generations, the covenant he made with Abraham, the oath he swore to Isaac. He confirmed it to Jacob as a decree, to Israel as an everlasting covenant. (Psalm 105:1-10)

One day I stumbled across this passage and realized that the years of Bible study that God had led me to do focused exactly on these themes – and here they were, recommended to me by Scripture! The Name of the LORD, the Covenant, his judgments, his works and miracles – these were the subjects he had led me to focus on in my studies. It was a great confirmation that God wanted me to learn about *him* when I study the Bible.

It's amazing how preachers and teachers can miss this point. ***The whole purpose of the Bible is to reveal God.*** God is on every page. There is no other book under Heaven given for this purpose. Whatever we learn and know about God comes solely from the Bible, and all books which supposedly teach us about God must get its information only from the Bible in order to claim the label "truth." So, when we study the Bible, if we come up with a point about who he is or what he does, we got the right point; otherwise we're missing the whole point.

I once attended a church where a supposedly conservative, evangelical pastor was preaching a series of sermons on the book of Ephesians. It surprised me to see him squirming around the data about God and Christ in this great book; to him, the book was a list of moralisms and do's and don'ts for the Christian life. "God" and "Christ" were simply sprinkled through the sermons but given no content at all. There was no lesson on what God did, or what Jesus did. So while he was preaching in this fashion, I made my own list of what Ephesians actually teaches about God and Christ. I found 100 distinct truths about God in this short book! Each one of these points about God that Paul gave us is a gold-mine of spiritual treasure, hope for the soul, strength and wisdom from Heaven.

On the other hand, if you teach the Bible as if it were a counseling session or opinions about current events, people will start to go dry spiritually. There's no hope in ourselves – no matter how hard we try. Like the farmer's seed planted in soil full of weeds, we can zealously live for God for a while, but then the cares of this world will take over our time and attention and prove just how shallow our faith really is – we will die in the end. To live spiritually, you need deep roots into Christ, who is our life.

Shallow Bible teaching doesn't satisfy the soul. Let's put it another way – to focus on man continually will make people dissatisfied and unfulfilled, still looking for and yet not finding what they need spiritually. They will end up going somewhere else where they will be fed. I once taught the purpose of the Bible to a group of college students. A couple of years later, one of the girls came back and told me this story. She and some friends of hers went to a conference held by a well-known national campus ministry, where a well-known speaker in the ministry came to teach. While her friends were enthusiastic about this speaker, my student found herself troubled by him for some reason. Something was missing. Then it occurred to her that *he was saying absolutely nothing about God* in this supposedly Bible-based, Christ-centered message! And the only reason she knew what was wrong was because she was trained to spot that fatal error.

Let's look at some examples of the knowledge of God in the Bible.

- **The Creator** – In Genesis we learn that God created the world. That in itself answers all sorts of questions. But we can learn more – for example, we see *how* God created it (we will see him using these same methods throughout the rest of the Bible), *why* he created it, what he expects out of it, and just exactly how we are to relate to him because of him being our Creator.

- **The Covenant** – God made an agreement with Abraham. In this agreement he promised to do four things for Abraham and his heirs. Those four things form the very basis of the Gospel that is preached in the New Testament! And we also learn who exactly is going to keep this Covenant alive and well through the centuries – and it's neither Abraham nor his descendants.

- **The Law** – When God led the Israelites out of Egypt, he brought them to Mt. Sinai and formed them into a nation. The Law that he gave them there was the legal framework for his government over them as their God and King. This Law not only gives us the world's only true definition of sin and righteousness, but it points to only one person who could keep the Law in its entirety – God himself! And that's why the Son of God came to fulfill the Law.

- **King David** – When David took over the throne of Israel from Saul, he inherited a kingdom in disorder. His job was to restore the Kingdom according to the guidelines of God. These guidelines form the foundation of the work that Jesus, the son of David, did in his own ministry as described in the Gospels.

- **The Prophets** – A prophet wasn't just someone who predicted future events. What made a man a prophet of God was *what* he predicted. The Prophet saw God coming from Heaven; he had a message from this God to deliver to God's people before the Lord arrived personally at the scene to exercise judgment. The message described what God intended to do to fix his broken Kingdom. We are told to "pay more attention to" the prophets (2 Peter 1:19), because on Judgment Day we too will stand before this God who knows the hearts of all men. Those old messages are aimed at us too.

- **Jesus** – Many people think that Jesus came simply to set an example for the rest of us on how to live in this world. Not so. He grappled with spiritual forces during his life; he pulled together the ancient themes of the Old Testament and raised them up to form a new spiritual Kingdom; he fulfilled the Abrahamic covenant; he left earth only to assume his new enlarged duties as King of kings at the right hand of the throne of God. The story of Jesus should convince us that we *can't* be like this man! That our only hope is that he will have mercy on us and do for us, and in us, what we can't do on our own.

- **The Apostles** – Jesus specially trained certain men to take the message of his life and work to the nations. That message, however, consisted of truths that the natural man would never have known on his own. It was the "mystery" of the Gospel – a unique vision of the spiritual side of Christ, the truth of the God-Man finally solving this problem of sin and death that holds the entire world in darkness. The Apostles were amazed and thrilled in what they were enabled to see in Christ, and they passed those insights on to us so that we might have their same faith in the Son of God.

- **The book of Revelation** – Just as an example of seeing the spiritual side of Jesus, the book of Revelation shows us things that we would have never guessed from reading only the Gospels! Here Jesus reigns as absolute ruler over the whole universe. Here he finally gets vengeance on his enemies. Here all our fears are put to rest – like what will happen to the faithful, whether there will be justice in the end, what will happen to all God's enemies, what kind of world Jesus is preparing for us, and what will happen to this first creation. Jesus is managing the entire thing for us.

Hopefully you can see that the Bible is full of the knowledge of God. All it takes is the determination to look for God in it. Don't leave the passage, don't think that you understand its true meaning, until you find out what it's saying about God.

I'm sure that some will object by saying that the Bible does talk about man and his duties and responsibilities. That's true – but only in context of the knowledge of God. We know what right and wrong are, we know our duties and responsibilities to God, only by looking at the holy God first. For example, the questions concerning sex and marriage in our society would clear up immediately if we study the Creation story and use it as the pattern for life. Here we are told what God did when he made us, what he told us to do, and why he did it.

Another example: remember that we saw that Ephesians teaches us 100 different facts about God. Notice that Paul waits for the "practical" side of Christianity until the last three chapters of the book. He first covers a great deal of material about Christ, our relationship to him, our privileges in Heaven because of him, and so on. Once this foundation is laid, he then goes on to our duties as children, husbands and wives, servants, and so on. Study this passage and you will begin to see why he advises us to live in such a way – it reflects what he said about our relationship to God through Christ in the first half. In other words, without that spiritual insight about God first, he could never have drawn the conclusions later about Christian life.

We also see the Apostle Peter looking at God and his works first, and then from that drawing certain conclusions concerning our way of living.

> Since everything will be destroyed in this way, what
> kind of people ought you to be? You ought to live holy
> and godly lives as you look forward to the day of God
> and speed its coming. (2 Peter 3:11-12)

A morality that doesn't first come out of the knowledge of God isn't going to work. Go ahead and tell people that they should love each other. It makes a nice theme, it's a nice ideal, but people will find that they can't do it in the long run. They neither want to love others nor do they have the ability to do so – particularly when circumstances get tense. But if you start with God first – that he is holy, that he is good, that we learn to love him because of who he is and what he does – this lays the foundation for love for others. We know what love is, John tells us, because Jesus first loved us.

> This is how we know what love is: Jesus Christ laid
> down his life for us. And we ought to lay down our lives
> for our brothers. (1 John 3:16)

No wonder then that John told us "if anyone says 'I love God' yet hates his brother, he is a liar!" (1 John 4:20) Love for your brother naturally comes out of the love for God – God's Spirit is a sweet aroma that unites the family of God and brings us into the presence of God through worship and fellowship.

A God-centered life

We are told plainly to learn more about God. Paul tells us this in Colossians.

> For this reason, since the day we heard about you,
> we have not stopped praying for you and asking God to
> fill you with the knowledge of his will through all
> spiritual wisdom and understanding. (Colossians 1:9)

The reason for this is more important than you think. You cannot live the Christian life as he wants you to unless you learn about God. You can't be good, you can't be holy, you can't love your neighbor, you can't even keep yourself away from sin, unless you learn more about God.

> And we pray this *in order that you may live a life
> worthy of the Lord and may please him in every way:*
> bearing fruit in every good work, *growing in the
> knowledge of God*, being strengthened with all power
> according to his glorious might so that you may have
> great endurance and patience, and joyfully giving thanks
> to the Father, who has qualified you to share in the
> inheritance of the saints in the kingdom of light.
> (Colossians 1:10-12)

While the rest of the world sits at the feet of false gods and false religions, learning their false systems of morality and ethics and values and getting nowhere, we Christians have the amazing opportunity to sit at God's feet and learn of him. Our way, unlike so many other paths in this world, leads to life. The secret is to get in touch with the one true God and learn as much of him as we can.

> Now this is eternal life: that they may know you, the only true God, and Jesus Christ, whom you have sent. (John 17:3)

A view of the entire Bible

A lot of the confusion that people have over the Bible is due to the fact that it's a huge book, with hundreds of characters, thousands of ideas, and no "summary page" to pull the whole thing together!

One thing that we can do is back way up and see the entire sweep of the Bible. To do this, we are going to ignore the man-made lines of division for a while. They tend to confuse the issue. For example, the "Old Testament" label was actually added to the Bible by the Church, after they had decided what the "New Testament" would be, centuries after Jesus lived. That artificial line between the two sections has caused no end of confusion and outright heresy over the millennia.

And though the Bible has 66 books, it's actually one story. That has been one of the most amazing aspects of the Bible – there have been so many human authors, working over thousands of years, yet the piece that each one gave us fits right into the whole picture! This makes us believe that there is really only one Author.

We're going to let the Bible draw its own lines – and the story naturally falls into three parts.

The Solution to our problem

The Bible is actually very simple. It deals with the fundamental problems of mankind in a perfectly clear manner. No matter how advanced our modern technological society gets, we still have the same basic needs in life. We also have the same basic shortcomings – which the Bible lays out for us plainly in many places.

When you boil down the Bible to its simplest level, it actually covers three things: the **Problem**, which describes why we have such a terrible relationship with the God who made us; the **Solution Described**, which shows how God intends to solve our problem for his glory and our eternal benefit; and the **Solution Applied**, in which God takes the finished plan and starts saving people from their problem.

The Problem	The Solution Described	The Solution Applied

Genesis 1-11	**Genesis 12 – John**	**Acts - Revelation**

 The Problem: Genesis 1-11

The Bible starts out by describing the fundamental problem of humanity. But in order to do this, it first starts with the Creation of the world. Here we learn *who* made the world, *how* he made it, and *why* he made it.

God made the world, we are told in Genesis, and we learn right away that he is holy and righteous. So he designed the entire world to show off his holiness – all his creatures are designed and expected to glorify him. He is also the King, ruling the universe from his throne in Heaven. This means that all creatures were made to serve him, according to his specific rules. His rules are what we call righteousness, or the Law.

There are more things about God that we can learn from Genesis, but just these two points are enough to set the background for the problem to come. In Genesis 3 we find out that Adam and Eve rebelled against the King and turned their back on his holiness. In that act of rebellion they brought down the entire human race into disaster. Now all of their children will inherit their sin nature. And God responded with a sentence of death as a just punishment against Adam and his race. Now instead of a happy communion between God and man, there is war. And there doesn't appear to be any chance of a reconciliation, since God closed the doors to Heaven and eternal life.

The problem gets worse – or perhaps we should say that we see the true extent and seriousness of the problem as the story unfolds. The first murder occurs in Genesis 4, teaching us what man is capable of doing to his fellow man out of selfishness and jealousy. In Genesis 6-9 we are told that all of humanity is wallowing in its sins; the situation was so bad that God decided to sweep the planet clean and start over with Noah (at least one person had true faith!) and his immediate family. Then in Genesis 11 we see the entire world back in sin, challenging God's authority over them, and building the Tower of Babel as a symbol of rebellion and independence. God scattered them over the whole earth and took away their ability to work together against him.

So the situation, described in the first 11 chapters of the Bible, is this: Heaven and earth are at war with each other, and there doesn't appear to be any hope that we're going to survive this war. Mankind is determined to rebel against God and have its own way; God is just as determined to stop man, wiping him out entirely if necessary, to stay in control of the situation. We have an impasse on our hands. If something isn't done, we're all doomed. But the only one who can make a move to break the impasse at this point is God.

We need Genesis 1-11 to show us the nature of the problem (treason against God), the extent of the problem (world-wide and in every human being), and how seriously God takes it (death is the punishment). At least we all know now where we stand with our Maker. And we know now that there's nothing *we* can do to fix the problem.

The Solution Described: Genesis 12 – John

There *is* a second solution to mankind's problem – besides wholesale destruction.   Without relaxing his standards, God introduced a way of forgiving our sin against him and delivering us from any further sin. He's going to re-open the way to the Tree of Life, but on his terms.

This solution is staggering, to say the least.   God is going to do things that people would never have imagined. Even the angels – who are God's messengers and closest to the Throne of Heaven – would be kept in the dark until the whole solution unfolds.   The job at hand is to completely free the sinner from condemnation, yet satisfy the righteous requirements of the Law, and make sure that sin would never happen again – the whole time changing man's heart so that he *wants* to cooperate with God in this venture. So the answer that God provides is going to be astonishing and complex; it's going to require thousands of years to complete.

The Lord described and worked out the solution in stages.   First came the Promise, the Covenant, with Abraham and his descendants – starting with Genesis 12. Through the entire history of the Jews (as described in the Old Testament), God worked out the Solution.   Keep in mind that he worked on parts of the solution at different periods of Israel's history, but the entire pattern is already complete in Heaven. There's never any doubt about where he's going. He knew from the beginning where he wanted to end up. We are shown no more than a glimpse of the solution in any particular story, but each bit is a precious and vital step in our salvation. To the perceptive Jew, the parts added up to a whole picture of God's salvation of mankind.

And another method that God used was the idea of "shadows." Instead of directly revealing the Kingdom of Heaven that will be our eternal home, he cast shadows of that spiritual world on the earth. The Jews had to work with those shadows, not the real thing. They were told about this, and they were expected to know that true faith would trust in the real spiritual world behind the physical land, the Temple, and the animal sacrifices. But the shadows played their role in the process of salvation, because we can more easily learn from what we see and feel than from invisible concepts.

What this means is that each thing that happened in the Old Testament wasn't an imperfect picture, but a piece of the picture. We need to put all the pieces together to see the whole picture. The New Testament isn't the mature statement over against the "childish" or immature religion of the Jews (as some critics claim). The New Testament simply goes back to the Old Testament, collects all the pieces, and lifts it up into God's spiritual world – a resurrection of sorts. The physical body becomes a spiritual body in the New Testament. And the Old Testament pattern, filled with the light of Christ, finally makes sense.

To truly understand the story of Jesus, we first need to do our homework in the history of the Israelites. He was symbolized in many forms, each of which teach us a different facet of the Son of God. For example, he is portrayed in the Passover meal in Exodus as the spotless Lamb offered for our sake so that we might not be destroyed. And Revelation 5 confirms him as a Lamb on the throne. Everyone knows that Jesus isn't a literal animal lamb; what we need to learn is *why* he is shown as a Lamb – and the answer is in the Old Testament.

Even when Jesus appeared in the Gospels, God was still working out the finishing touches of the system. People were supposed to watch and learn, but the time had not yet come when they would experience the full weight of the power of God's salvation in their hearts. They could only wait for that reality.

The Solution Applied: Acts – Revelation

When Jesus said from the cross, "It is finished," he was speaking of the great system that God had been putting together in the Bible until that moment. Now the time had come to start applying the salvation that the Old Testament describes in the hearts of individuals.

We find out right away that God meant it to be a spiritual solution. He did away with the physical that he used to teach the Israelites; they must now grow up and start thinking in spiritual terms. The blood of bulls and goats, we are told, never was enough to cleanse our hearts of sin. It was only meant to teach us the utter seriousness of sin (death is the penalty), and God's mercy in providing an alternate victim for our sin. And so God destroyed the Temple, the sacrificial system, everything that the Jews were relying on for their salvation.

Also we learn the method that God is going to use to pull off what couldn't be done even in the Old Testament days. Though the Israelites had learned the truth of God's plan of salvation, they still lacked the motive power – they remained sinners after all their prayers and sacrifices. But now Jesus will send his Holy Spirit to live inside us. That power will bring about the heart-change that God requires of his people. God's people – even from the Old Testament days – have longed for this step.

There are a lot of things that the Holy Spirit will enable us to do. All these things were first described in the Old Testament, of course. The Spirit will enable us to ascend to the Throne of God in Heaven, enter his Temple, and present our prayers and requests to him. The Spirit will break our hearts of stone and move us to follow his decrees and laws. The Spirit will defend us from our enemies. The Spirit will bring us to a land of peace, fill our lives with "milk and honey," and make us a testimony to the nations surrounding us. What the Jews wished they could do but couldn't, Christians now are able to do.

The end result is astonishing. In Christ, who has gone before us (he makes every single step in this process work for us), we will ascend to the throne of God himself as priests and sit at his right hand as his children. There we will rule over his new Heavens and earth *as we were designed to do at the beginning.* But there won't be any second fall into sin and death. Being one with the Son of God, we will be pure and holy forever. And we will actually *like* it that way!

By looking at the Bible in this way – **Problem**, **Solution Described**, and **Solution Applied** – we get a feel for God's great work of salvation throughout history. It's one project, one plan, bringing all of God's people into his eternal Kingdom. Paul describes it like this:

There is one body and one Spirit – just as you were called to one hope when you were called – one Lord, one faith, one baptism; one God and Father of all, who is over all and through all and in all. (Ephesians 4:4-6)

We know of course that history consists of much more than the Bible's narrow focus. After reading Greek history, and Roman history, and the full history of the Egyptians, and the history of Medieval Europe, and all of modern history, we realize that the little bit of history that the Bible talks about is actually a miniscule part of all human endeavor. Most of humanity, unfortunately, will never know the blessings that are described in the Bible's story of salvation. The Bible is not their story. God has another plan for those who take the "wide road" of sin – the terrible day of Judgment and the Lake of Fire.

But for a few, the Bible describes their future – it's about God providing a way of escape from the day of wrath. While the rest of the world concerns itself with *this* world which eventually will be destroyed, the children of God are following a different track – they are being preparing for life in the *new* world in Heaven that the Bible describes.

Physical and Spiritual Levels

We mentioned it above, but the point bears more study. One of the most important aspects of the Bible is how the physical and spiritual levels interact with each other in the timeline of God's works.

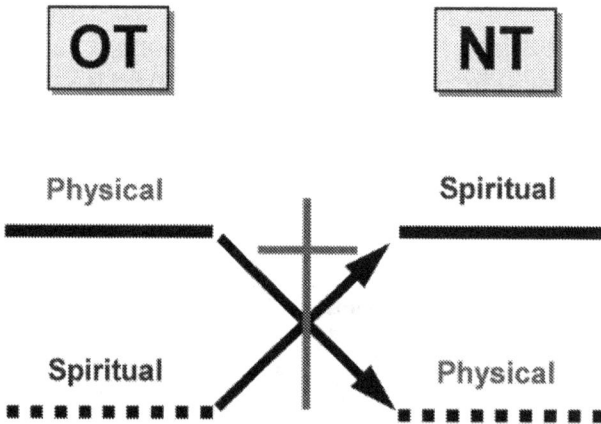

Figure 6 – Physical & Spiritual Levels

- In the **Old Testament**, the *physical* level predominates. We see animal sacrifices in a physical Temple. We see the children of Israel settling down in Canaan. We watch David pulling the tribes together and defeating the Moabites and Philistines. Just about everything we read about is something that we can see, feel, or hear with our physical senses.

God did this for a reason. Since the solution to mankind's problems of sin and death is so complex – and since the ultimate solution is a spiritual one which nobody can see – he started out by teaching us the answer on a level that we could easily grasp. It's amazing how much children can learn if you make your point in the form of stories and pictures.

So to teach us lessons of his spiritual world in terms that we cannot mistake the meaning of, he used stories of his works in the lives of real people in real places. The point is there for anybody to see; a child can understand the story; and if we read and believe what God is saying, we can be saved.

Some of the important stories of the Bible include the following:

The Creation of the world
Abel's sacrifice
The Flood
The Covenant with Abraham
The Blessing of Jacob
Deliverance through Joseph
The Exodus
The Promised Land
David and Solomon
The Divided Kingdom
Punishment and Exile
Rebuilding the Temple and the walls of Jerusalem

We miss the point if we think that these events (and many others) were merely physical events that happened to the Jews only. The Bible was written for all of us; the whole Church is the recipient of God's letter. The physical events recorded in the Old Testament describe the same things that happen in God's spiritual world *in all ages.*

Yet we also catch a glimpse of the spiritual just behind the physical, right underneath the surface, if we have the eyes to see and ears to hear. Passages like the following show us that God always did consider the physical level to be temporary and not the ultimate point:

> "The multitude of your sacrifices – what are they to me?" says the LORD. "I have more than enough of burnt offerings, of rams and the fat of fattened animals; I have no pleasure in the blood of bulls and lambs and goats." (Isaiah 1:11)

Didn't he tell the Israelites to bring these sacrifices to him at the Temple? Yet here he is claiming that he doesn't want them! The point is that they were hiding behind the animal sacrifice as if that would cleanse their souls, and then going right back into their sin. This is not the way to worship God! The sacrifices were designed to teach us how terrible is the effect of sin. We're supposed to stop our sinning. If anything, the sacrifice would point up the need for something more permanent that would change the heart, so that we wouldn't sin anymore. The sacrifices of the Temple were an embarrassing reminder of the weakness of the system.

Paul also gives us clues that some of the Old Testament saints understood the ultimate point of a spiritual kingdom.

> A man is not a Jew if he is only one outwardly, nor is circumcision merely outward and physical. No, a man is a Jew if he is one inwardly; and circumcision is circumcision of the heart, by the Spirit, not by the written code. Such a man's praise is not from men, but from God. (Romans 2:28-29)

> The LORD your God will circumcise your
> hearts and the hearts of your descendants, so
> that you may love him with all your heart and
> with all your soul, and live. (Deuteronomy
> 30:6)

• In the **New Testament**, the *spiritual* level
predominates. The situation flip-flops, so to speak. Now
instead of a physical Temple, we learn of the Temple in
Heaven that we must come to. Now instead of a physical
land of Canaan to inherit, we inherit Heaven. David
sitting on throne in Jerusalem turns into the Son of David
sitting on his throne beside the Father. The Philistines
aren't a problem to us anymore, but our sins and the
"spiritual forces of darkness" certainly are.

Of course the situation in the Old Testament was also
spiritual, but they were required to learn and work things
out through the physical means that God gave them. Only
by faith would they realize that a more permanent solution
would eventually come to light. Now, however, the veil
has been taken away, the time has come; the eternal
solution has been revealed to us.

The Gentiles need to learn the lessons of the Old
Testament so that they can understand their faith. The
Jews need to graduate from their physical system so that
they can finally enjoy the reality of God's salvation.
Either way, we don't need the physical anymore. It has
served its purpose; the lessons are now recorded in the Old
Testament for all to learn. Those lessons are a stepping
stone, a primer to something better. Why long for the
shadow when you can have the real thing? That's why the
Apostles urged us to leave the physical behind and,
through faith, reach out for the eternal realities:

> The blood of goats and bulls and the ashes
> of a heifer sprinkled on those who are
> ceremonially unclean sanctify them so that

they are outwardly clean. How much more, then, will the blood of Christ, who through the eternal Spirit offered himself unblemished to God, cleanse our consciences from acts that lead to death, so that we may serve the living God! (Hebrews 9:13-14)

We do have a few minor physical aspects to our religion, however. We gather together in church buildings, we are baptized with water, we eat bread and drink wine at the communion service, we have preachers and teachers who train us with the Word of God. But we understand (or we're supposed to!) that these can't touch the soul like the Holy Spirit can. The reality isn't in the things we use in our religion; those are "vessels" through which God touches us with the treasures from Heaven. We know now that we can pray anywhere, not just in Jerusalem – because the Spirit lifts us up to the Throne of Heaven.

Our list that we used above – the physical items that God used to lead Israel – is still important to us, but now on a spiritual level.

The Creation of the world	*The New Creation*
Abel's sacrifice	*The sacrifice of Christ*
The Flood	*This world will be destroyed*
The Covenant with Abraham	*The Gospel of Christ*
The Blessing of Jacob	*Treasures in Heaven*
Deliverance through Joseph	*Deliverance through Christ*
The Exodus	*Leaving the world behind*
The Promised Land	*Heaven*
David and Solomon	*King Jesus*
The Divided Kingdom	*Division in the Church*
Punishment and Exile	*Discipline of God's people*
Rebuilding the Temple and the walls of Jerusalem	*Building the Church*

Remember that this list is a short one; there are so many lessons to be learned in the Old Testament and they all have spiritual counterparts in Christ's Kingdom. God's Kingdom used to be on earth, among the Jews, and they first learned what it's like to live with this God. Now the Church is living with him, and they too must learn the same lessons. The difference is that we are in training for living with a spiritual God that we can't see or touch.

Angels versus Christ

Keep in mind that God had the same agenda in both the physical and spiritual systems. We find the following works of God in both Testaments:

- Revelation
- Redemption
- Deliverance
- Protection
- Direction
- Discipline

In the Old Testament, God did this work through angels (see Hebrews 1 for this discussion). Angels were usually on the scene when God worked on the earth: through angels God delivered messages to Abraham and Hagar, destroyed Sodom and Gomorrah, delivered Lot, led the Israelites through the wilderness, and so on. But angels are themselves created beings. "He makes his angels winds; his servants flames of fire." (Hebrews 1:7) So during the entire Old Testament ministry, God worked with his people through, or by means of, created things.

In the New Testament (which includes our times) he now does *this same work* through Christ. The work through angels was temporary and couldn't change the heart, or really fix the problem that man has. The work done through Christ is effective and eternal. When he reveals the truth, it aims for the heart and our spiritual senses are opened to spiritual truths. When he delivers us from sin, our hearts are cleansed and we don't sin again. Jesus actually does what the angels could never hope to do. The promise is in the Old Testament, and the fulfillment is in the New. As the writer of Hebrews says,

> These were all commended for their faith, yet none of them received what had been promised. God had planned something better for us so that only together with us would they be made perfect. (Hebrews 11:39-40)

And this is a preview of what it's going to be like in Heaven. All the old Creation will be swept away (Hebrews 1:11-12) and replaced with a new Heaven and earth. We will no longer be blessed through created things (all that will be gone), and God will no longer use angels or creation to reach us. Instead he will touch us directly with his hand; we will live before his face; we will hear and see God, and enjoy *him* forever.

Another way we can show this is by the following chart:

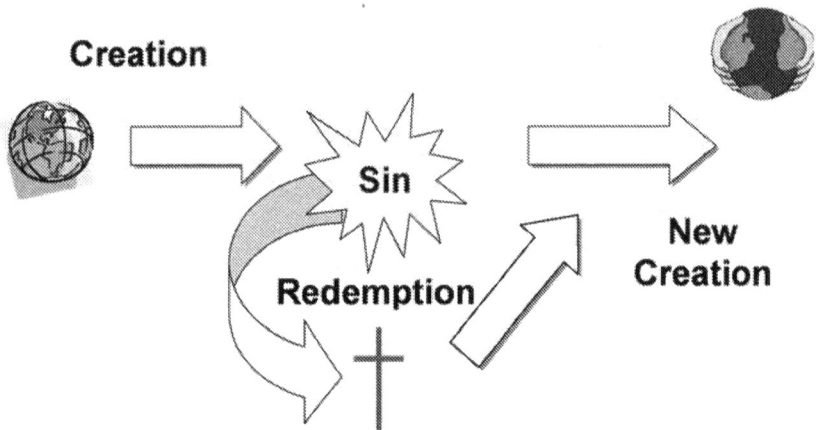

Figure 7 – Redeeming Creation

In the beginning, God created a perfect world and had every intention of blessing man and enabling him to rule over his earth in his Name. Sin, however, blew apart that arrangement. God refused to go on in such circumstances. But rather than simply do away with the whole thing and call it quits, he took an alternate route – one in which he would personally suffer on our account, but a few of us would be saved from the disaster that mankind brought upon itself. Once Jesus bought reconciliation with God through his death, and opened the way to eternal life through his resurrection, man was brought back to his Maker (and his Redeemer!) and set back on the path to eternal life. When everyone that God saves is brought back to him, he will put them in a new Heaven and earth where they will live with God forever, as originally planned. Only now there won't be any chance of going back to sin and death, because God will have his hands on us – we will be safe in Christ – forever.

Old and New Testaments

For a little while we had to set aside the distinction between "Old" and "New" Testaments, so that we could get the full picture of the Bible. It's really one story, not two. Now we want to draw the line between them again, but this time we're not going to set one against another but see how one complements the other. They are like two sides of the same coin.

Old and New

The line between them has been really unfortunate in that it causes many people to think that there are two stories in the Bible, or (as some seem to think) even two Gods! The God of the Old Testament, some say, is nothing like the God of the New Testament. Therefore many of those people simply ignore the Old Testament as being totally irrelevant to modern Christians. Why should we take seriously a blood-thirsty God who sent his people in war against their neighbors? Jesus taught a Gospel of peace, of the Spirit, and that fits better with our modern needs.

Another unfortunate idea came about over a passage in Hebrews. Many people think that this teaches a contrast, almost a contradiction, between the Old and New Testaments.

> But the ministry Jesus has received is as superior to theirs as the covenant of which he is mediator is superior to the old one, and it is founded on better promises. For if there had been nothing wrong with that first covenant, no place would have been sought for another. But God found fault with the people and said: "The time is coming, declares the Lord, when I will make a new covenant with the house of Israel and with the house of Judah." (Hebrews 8:6-8)

And then to nail the coffin shut they quote this passage ...

By calling this covenant "new," he has made the first one obsolete; and what is obsolete and aging will soon disappear. (Hebrews 8:13)

The word "covenant" in Greek (which is what the writer of Hebrews was using) can also be translated as "testament." So here we have, seemingly, all the justification we need to turn away from the Old Covenant or Testament in favor of the New Covenant or Testament.

And that seems to fit in with Paul's tirade against legalists, especially in Galatians. We know that the Israelites received the Law of God in the Old Testament – and Paul says that following the Law is bad. Jesus, in the New Testament, calls us with the Gospel and faith in him – and that's good. So, again, Christians seemingly are called away from the legalistic Old Testament so that they can live by faith in the teaching of the New Testament Gospel of Christ.

I used the word "seemingly" because this is a superficial way of looking at the Bible. For example, let's go back to that idea of old and new covenants. To get the real meaning of the Hebrews passage, we have to keep reading. The next verse explains the problem.

It will not be like the covenant I made with their forefathers when I took them by the hand to lead them out of Egypt, because they did not remain faithful to my covenant, and I turned away from them, declares the Lord. This is the covenant I will make with the house of Israel after that time, declares the Lord. *I will put my laws in their minds and write them on their hearts.* I will be their God, and they will be my people. (Hebrews 8:9-10)

If you know something about Old Testament history, you will recognize this reference to the Exodus and Mt. Sinai. God brought his people out of Egypt and made them his nation; he would be their God, and they would obey his Law. At Mt. Sinai he gave them his Law through Moses. There was nothing wrong with the Law – it was a perfect statement of God's holiness and the kind of life that he expected out of his people. Without the Law there would be utter chaos in his Kingdom, as there would be in any kingdom that is lawless. The difficulty of the Law is seen in this passage:

> And if we are careful to obey ***all*** this Law before the LORD our God, as he has commanded us, ***that*** will be our righteousness. (Deuteronomy 6:25)

Righteousness is the qualification for living in God's Kingdom. If you're righteous, you can stay; if you're not righteous, then you must be punished or eliminated. At Mt. Sinai, what the Israelites learned is that they must follow this Law to the letter if they wanted to be counted righteous. And as they proved so eloquently in their subsequent travels, that's impossible! Nobody can follow this Law perfectly. There's only one man in history that has successfully followed the Law to the letter, and that's Christ himself. The rest of us simply can't live up to that high standard. Yet God will never relax the standard, because he won't put up with a Kingdom full of unrighteous subjects.

But if someone can *make* us righteous, that would also satisfy God's requirement. This is in fact what Jesus does for us. He takes the burden of obedience to the Law from our backs, fulfills the Law in our place, and then gives us his righteousness as a gift. Now we can freely enter God's Kingdom without fear of rejection.

But he also must make provision for our continuing in righteousness, so he fills us with his Spirit to drive us, mold us, move us to live according to God's Law. We can't do it on our own, but Jesus, as he lives in our hearts, will draw us after him in conformity to the Law of God – so that we will never be rejected.

And that is what it means when Hebrews says, "I will put my laws in their minds and write them on their hearts." The Law has not changed, nor has the requirement to live according to the Kingdom Law changed. What has changed is this: who is going to make this happen in us? The Israelites themselves had to follow the Law, and they failed; we Christians rely on Christ to conform us to God's Law. The end result is the same – perfect righteousness – but the means is different. Only the Christian can achieve perfect righteousness by the Law's standard.

The Prophets longed for this day:

> I will give you a new heart and put a new spirit in you; I will remove from you your heart of stone and give you a heart of flesh. And I will put my Spirit in you and *move you to follow my decrees and be careful to keep my laws*. (Ezekiel 36:26-27)

Paul, who had a profound understanding of both the Law and Christ, never set the two in contradiction. He had a high respect for the Law. But he also knew that we could never keep the Law on our own. The solution is that Jesus would keep the Law for our sake and change us to satisfy the Law's requirements.

> Therefore, there is now no condemnation for those who are in Christ Jesus, because through Christ Jesus the law of the Spirit of life set me free from the law of sin and death. For what the Law was powerless to do in that it was weakened by the sinful nature, God did by sending his own Son in the likeness of sinful man to be a sin offering. And so he condemned sin in sinful man, *in order that the righteous requirements of the Law might be fully met in us*, who do not live according to the sinful nature but according to the Spirit. (Romans 8:1-4)

So, the Old and New Testaments aren't contrary to each other, nor do they teach different doctrine. The contrast in Hebrews 8 isn't referring to the "Old and New Testaments" as they are called in our Bibles. The contrast is in how the Israelites were to achieve righteousness and how we are to achieve it. They were supposed to follow all the Law's requirements; we trust in Jesus to do it for us. And as we shall see, the way of faith actually predates the Law in Abraham, which means that God always did mean for us to do this through Christ!

The Point of the Old Testament

As we've just seen, it's wrong to say that the Old Testament is the "Law" and the New Testament is the "Gospel." The Law is integral to the New Testament story, and the Gospel is fully outlined in the Old Testament story. Abraham first learned about the Gospel of Christ, and Paul was anxious to see the requirements of the Law in our hearts. So we can't continue to set one side of the Bible against the other one.

But each side has its purpose; there is a line of sorts, which the life of Christ made real. And it relates to what we've already seen about the Bible. Now that Christ has come, all the hopes and promises that we learned from God in the Old Testament are going to be fulfilled in us. Now that we've learned about our fundamental problem and what God's answer is going to be, the New Testament opens the veil in Heaven and starts bringing us into eternal life.

But before we start taking advantage of God's answer, let's first look at the description of it in the Old Testament. Here is where God lays out the blueprints for the solution of man's problem of sin and death.

One thing we must do, however, is read the Old Testament in the way that God wants us to read it. If we don't, we will miss its point entirely. For example, the one reason that the Jews, even to this day, do not understand their own Scriptures is because they refuse to study it from God's perspective.

> You diligently study the Scriptures because you think that by them you possess eternal life. ***These are the Scriptures that testify about me***, yet you refuse to come to me to have life. (John 5:39-40)

> But do not think I will accuse you before the Father. Your accuser is Moses, on whom your hopes are set. If you believed Moses, you would believe me, ***for he wrote about me***. But since you do not believe what he wrote, how are you going to believe what I say? (John 5:45-47)

I know that there are Biblical scholars (Christian ones, too!) who believe that it's not fair to impose a Christian interpretation on the Old Testament. They think that we have to let the Jewish Scriptures speak for themselves, without using "rose-colored glasses" to find the "real" meaning of their book. But we can't go by what the scholars think; we have to go by what God says to do. Jesus plainly says here that the Old Testament teaches about *him* – if we don't see him in its pages, then we're not reading it correctly. Paul makes an equally strong statement about this.

> But as for you, continue in what you have learned and have become convinced of, because you know those from whom you learned it, and how from infancy you have known the holy Scriptures, *which are able to make you wise for salvation through faith in Christ Jesus*. (1 Timothy 3:14-15)

Paul, of course, was referring to the only "Scriptures" they had at that time – what we call the Old Testament. And in his estimation, the Old Testament was a workbook on Christ – this is what he used to teach people about the truth of Christ. But in order to make that kind of statement about the Old Testament, he had to see it as not just a collection of prophecies about the coming Messiah (which is the most that many people today can say about it) but a full description of the Messiah's work and person. He says here that we can be *saved in Christ* by studying the Old Testament – what many thought was strictly a New Testament concept!

Even the Jews were supposed to approach their Scriptures with faith – which would enable them to see the same spiritual point that we Christians see there. They were in fact expected to see Jesus in their religion.

One more point that we have to make here is that God had all this business of salvation worked out from the beginning of time. He didn't make this up as he went along. God is all-knowing, he controls all, and nothing surprises him. He anticipated man's fall into sin and death with a complete system of salvation even before Adam fell into sin.

So was fulfilled what was spoken through the prophet: "I will open my mouth in parables, I will utter things hidden *since the creation of the world.*" (Matthew 13:35)

Then the King will say to those on his right, "Come, you who are blessed by my Father; take your inheritance, the kingdom prepared for you *since the creation of the world.*" (Matthew 25:34)

For he chose us in him *before the creation of the world* to be holy and blameless in his sight. (Ephesians 1:4)

He was chosen *before the creation of the world*, but was revealed in these last times for your sake. (1 Peter 1:20)

All inhabitants of the earth will worship the beast – all whose names have not been written in the book of life belonging to the Lamb that was slain *from the creation of the world.* (Revelation 13:8)

This certainly puts the Old Testament in a new light. We can expect to see details of the Gospel of Christ at the very beginning of the story – which we indeed find in the story of Abraham. It's not that God worked out the details as he worked with the Israelites; rather, he let them in on the details in stages. He knew all along what the full picture would be.

Now we can state the purpose of the Old Testament, since we've laid the necessary foundation for how to study it.

**The Old Testament describes Christ,
and our relationship to God the Father through him.**

The point of the Old Testament is Christ, as Jesus himself claimed. In light of the root problem of mankind, we need help if we're ever going to have a positive relationship with the God who made us. Jesus is that key to our restoration. God has provided a way to reconcile us to himself, to erase the past horrors, and yet to satisfy the requirements of the Law. And he plans to restore us not only to our former glory of rulers over his Creation, but a greater glory of rulers of his Creation from his own throne. All this is to be accomplished through Christ.

When you think about it, this is a staggering concept. Its agenda, its scope, its complexity, and the necessary power to pull it off is beyond human imagination. God certainly didn't choose the easy route when he decided to *restore* man instead of destroying him!

The solution itself, then, is going to require a great deal of explanation in order to fully describe it in all its details. The subject of Christ is huge. Just a list of his Names, which describe his person and work, runs to over 125 entries! Names describe things and people, and Christ's Names describe the many kinds of work that he does for his people.

There are many different facets of Christ's work that we don't want to miss. Like a diamond that has facets, or cut surfaces, that reflect its beauty, Jesus has many aspects that show off his glory and power.

We need a lot of room to go into depth about God's solution to sin and death. And it would help to make the explanation simple enough for anybody to understand. Furthermore, let's break it down so that we're not overwhelmed by the complexity of the thing – let's have it one point at a time.

The Old Testament does exactly this for us. It spreads out the explanation of Christ over two thousand years, throughout the lives of millions of people, across 39 books – one story at a time. Though we're not told this at the beginning of each of the stories, we could preface them all by saying "Now this is another aspect of Christ." The clue that we're not only allowed to do this but required to is the plain teaching of the New Testament about the purpose of the Old.

Let's look at some examples.

• In the **Creation** account of Genesis, we see God making the world through three methods: through his *Word*, by means of *miracles*, and by *command*. This is so important that many of the other Old Testament writers returned to the idea again and again. The saints continually called on the Creator God who created the world in this way – because the answers they needed at the time of their crisis required the same kind of methods that God used at the beginning. (See 2 Kings 19:14-19; Nehemiah 9:6; Acts 4:24-30)

What is fascinating is that Jesus worked with the same three methods! In the Gospel accounts he does the same work as the Creator in Genesis did, *in the same way*. And there are reasons for God using these particular methods which only Christians can fully appreciate – the eternal Church depends on *this kind* of foundation. This should tell us that we're looking at the same God in Christ that we read about in the Old Testament. No wonder, then, that Paul says that God created the world through Christ. (Colossians 1:16-17)

• In the story of the **Covenant with Abraham**, God promises to do four things for Abraham and his heirs: *first*, to give him a son through a miracle; *second*, to give them the land Canaan to live in; *third*, to make his family a great nation; and *fourth*, to bless the world through him and his family. There was an immediate fulfillment for each of these promises (for example, the boy Isaac was the fulfillment of the first promise) but even Abraham knew that there was a greater spiritual fulfillment for each point. Jesus taught that "your father Abraham rejoiced at the thought of seeing my day; he saw it and was glad." (John 8:56)

The promises to Abraham can be described like this: *first*, God promised a **Son** born by miracle, an heir of all the promises given to Abraham. He would see to it that the family of God would live by faith, would enjoy all the covenant blessings, and walk in holiness as required by the covenant. That Son was Christ himself.

Second, God promised a **Land** for his people to live in. It would have to be a perfect land, one in which God would richly bless his people and they would live in his presence. Heaven is that eternal home.

Third, God promised that Abraham's heirs would become a great **nation** – one that would extend all around the globe, and even cross the Jewish-Gentile barrier that the Jews thought couldn't be violated. The Church is the family that God has in mind for eternity.

Fourth, the **blessing** that God promised to the world through Abraham's line is the reversal of the curse on mankind, or death – which will be resurrection from the dead. God is going to reverse the old curse that kept us from the Tree of Life and give his people eternal life.

Each of these four points are expanded, symbolized, and described in various aspects of Israel's history – in the Temple, for example, with its symbols of forgiveness and living with God. The covenant with Abraham ruled the history of the Jews at every stage.

But you can hopefully see the Gospel of the New Testament in that covenant as well! What more would you want from God, as a Christian, than Christ as your Lord, the promise of Heaven, the family of the Church, and eternal life? This is our faith carefully woven into the fabric of the story of the Old Testament, passed down to us from our father Abraham. Abraham himself, according to testimony from the New Testament, understood the spiritual realities of each of these promises. To top it off, only those who can prove a family relationship with Abraham (the family characteristic is the *faith* that Abraham had – see Romans 4) can make any claim to the Gospel promises!

• The story of **Joseph**, though nowhere in the Bible are we told this in so many words, is a perfect picture of Christ's protection of his people. Through dreams and prophecies it was predicted that he would become the greatest member of his family. He suffered persecution at his brothers' hands. He was sold into the hands of his enemies, who put him into prison (the symbol of the grave). By edict of the Pharaoh he was brought out of death into life to sit at the King's right hand, second in command. From that position he ruled over the land in the King's name. He saved his family from the disaster of the famine and brought them to live with him in Egypt. And he not only forgave his brothers for their sin against him, but comforted and honored them with the blessings of the land. Here are many unexpected turns and twists in the story of Joseph that find an exact parallel in the ministry of Christ – which in fact shed a great deal of light on how Christ protects his people.

• The **Law** describes the Perfect Man. As it says in the Law itself, whoever follows this Law to the letter will be perfect, righteous in God's eyes. It's another way of describing the holiness of God: if you want to live with this God, you must live in this way. Heaven is a place where the Law of God is honored and kept perfectly by all; it's what the Kingdom of God is all about.

The practical aspect of the Law is that it thoroughly condemns sinners. Any deviation from the Law is sin, rebellion against God's plain command. As it says in the New Testament, "Everyone who sins breaks the Law; in fact, sin is lawlessness." (1 John 3:4) And it says in James that "whoever keeps the whole Law and yet stumbles at just one point is guilty of breaking all of it." (James 2:10) We have all broken the Law at some point or another. This means that we no longer have the option of trying to keep the Law to please God, or to attain a state of righteousness. It's too late for us now; the Law must now decide what to do with us law-breakers. The entire history of the Israelites revolves around this attempt to keep the Law and their failure to keep it.

The lesson to be learned from this is that we need someone else who can keep the Law for us! Jesus fulfilled the Old Testament Law perfectly, to the letter – for our sake. The Law didn't go away when Christ came; it found in him the only Man who could keep it. God has waited for a long time to see a man obey his Law! Our Christian lives now consist of Christ applying the fruits of his righteousness to our hearts, to conform us (by the power of his Spirit in us) to the righteous requirements of the Law. We don't have to try to obey the Law now; but as we *follow him* we will satisfy the Law's demands on us.

• When the Israelites arrived at the **Promised Land**, Joshua led them in to rid the land of Canaanites and settle the tribes into their new homes. The name "Joshua" is the Hebrew form of the Greek name "Jesus" – for a good reason. They both led their people in to take the land; they both waged war against the enemy to exterminate them; they both went in with the power of God with complete success. Joshua saw that the Israelites were settled in their new homes, and Jesus goes to prepare a place for his people in his Father's home.

The Promised Land is a description of what it's like to live with God. It's a rich land, a land "flowing with milk and honey," full of the treasures of the goodness of

God. Houses are already built, there is no more war, peace prevails over every household – and the glory of God dwells with his people. He rules from his throne over the whole land in righteousness. Everyone obeys the Lord's commands and prospers. It's what the original Creation was supposed to be.

• The **Temple** is a deep and perfect description of the work of Christ in Heaven for our sake. The earthly Temple was the scene for two important realities: *first*, the presence of God. Here he had his throne, here he sat to rule over his people, and here they could come to speak to their God. In other words, he lived among his people. This means that they had access to a living God, a God they could both know and hear and talk to. He wasn't like the idols of other nations, which couldn't speak or do anything. Israel's God proved his reality by his works among them.

Second, the Temple sacrifices made it possible for sinners to approach a holy God. Unless this problem was taken care of, God would have remained hidden from man and there would be no hope of reconciliation between the two. Man would die for his sins, and God would sweep away this evil world and probably go work on some other project. But a sacrifice satisfied the demand of the Law that someone must die for sin. It's God's mercy that he allowed a substitute instead of requiring *our* death.

The Temple in Heaven runs the same way that the earthly Temple ran. There must be a sacrifice before we're allowed into God's presence – the death of Christ. There still must be incense burning – the prayers of the saints. There still must be priests officiating, offering up petitions for God's people and carrying God's blessings and answers back to the people – Jesus the High Priest, and we who are Christians and called to serve him in his Temple as priests. In other words, the entire story of the

Temple was to get us used to the fact that we now must approach God in his Temple in Heaven, according to his rules, if we hope to get anything from him.

• **David** the king is the model for all the kings who followed him, including Jesus the Son of David. When David became king, he had five tasks to accomplish. *First*, he had to set up Jerusalem as his capital city. *Second*, he had to put an end to the threat of Israel's enemies. *Third*, he had to set up a government that would pull all of Israel's tribes together. *Fourth*, he had to lead the people back to God and true worship. *Fifth*, he had to lay out the plans for the Temple, where God would live among his people. Because David did these things faithfully, God called him a "man after my own heart." (1 Samuel 13:14)

All the kings who followed David were judged according to this standard that David set. "He did as his father David had done …" "He did not do as his father David had done …" Their task, as kings over God's people, was to enforce the rule of God and build up the Kingdom of God. A lot of the history of the Old Testament is a commentary on how each king handled this responsibility, or what happened when they didn't take it to heart.

When Jesus came he was called "the Son of David." This wasn't an empty title. In ascending to David's throne over God's Kingdom, Jesus was obligated by the job requirements to *do as his father David had done*. If you study the ministry of Christ with a keen eye, you will see him carefully following the same five steps that David first worked out. A lot of the work of Christ can be explained in this light.

As you can see, there are a lot of facts in the Old Testament concerning what it's like to live with God. We could go on and on. The Prophets came to warn us of an angry God who is tired of his

Kingdom being ruined by sin and idolatry; repent now, because the King is coming with an army to set things right again! The Redeemer (see the book of Ruth), at great cost to himself, pays the price to redeem his people to himself and marry them. The theme of God and his Bride can be found in several Old Testament books. Deliverance is a continual theme because his people need deliverance many times and in many ways. The Judge pierces the façade of the heart and requires purity and perfection on the part of his people; his eyes of fire penetrate the thoughts and attitudes of the heart. This is what it's like to live with God, both on earth and in Heaven.

Everywhere we look in the Old Testament we see another truth about Christ, another facet of his work, another precious treasure that will save us and make us ready to live with this holy God. If we gather all of these pictures and pieces together and make a whole story, the Name over all of it is **Jesus Christ**. The portrait that it paints is that of Christ. If we only go by what we manage to learn from the New Testament, we're going to see very little of the depth of Christ, very little of the vast scope of his work for our sake. We will miss out on the ins and outs of the relationship to God that Christ bought for us.

The Jews missed it entirely. It is entirely possible to miss the connection between Old Testament description of Christ and the New Testament Jesus – and they proved that unfortunate truth. Though they had the data of the Old Testament, they didn't realize that all their hopes and dreams had now come in flesh and blood ready to lift them up to the spiritual world that the Old had described for them.

We must not make the same mistake.

The Point of the New Testament

The Old Testament does such a good job at laying out the truths of the Kingdom of God that there is really very little left for the New Testament to cover. Like David who drew up the blueprints for the Temple and then instructed Solomon to carry out his orders, Jesus came simply to carry out his Father's will – which was plainly set out for him already in the Hebrew Scriptures.

We first learned about sacrifice for sins in the Old Testament. We learned about true faith in the story of Abraham. The Law taught us what God expects of those who want to live with him; it's the perfect description of righteousness. Resurrection from the dead can be found in several places in the Old Testament. The saints of that time knew (at least those who had faith!) that the Kingdom that God is really interested in is a spiritual Kingdom, not a physical one. The Temple in Heaven was fully described by the Temple on earth. We learned about the Redeemer in the Old, and the Deliverer, and the High Priest. We see the work of the Holy Spirit in the Old Testament.

Even the name "Jesus" is first found in the Old Testament. "Joshua" is the Hebrew equivalent of the Greek name "Jesus." Of course there were several people who had the name Joshua in Old Testament times simply because it was a popular name (just as many Hispanics bear the name "Jesus" in our day). But the Joshua who led the Israelites into the Promised Land didn't bear his name by accident; it was a preview of things to come in the spiritual Kingdom of God. Both names, in fact, come from an ancient Name of God that best described the God of Israel – "Jesus" is a combination of the words "Yahweh saves." It is first defined for us in Exodus 34:6-7, the first and best description in the Bible of how the God of love deals with sinners.

What is even more fascinating is that the Old Testament describes the special work that Jesus would do as Priest and King – one man carrying both responsibilities.

> Take the silver and gold and make a crown, and set it on the head of the high priest, Joshua son of Jehozadak. Tell him this is what the LORD Almighty says: "Here is the man whose name is the Branch, and he will branch out from his place and build the temple of the LORD. It is he who will build the temple of the LORD, and he will be clothed with majesty and will sit and rule on his throne. And he will be a priest on his throne. ***And there will be harmony between the two***." (Zechariah 6:11-13)

So we are taught that in Jesus both functions will come together – priest and king. In former days, the king of Israel came from the tribe of Judah, and the priest from the tribe of Levi. But if Jesus takes on the responsibility for both jobs, that would have raised some eyebrows among the legalists who want to see the organization run according to the Book. But by God's decree here in Zechariah *one* man *will* be both Priest and King, and his Name will be called – Jesus!

There are actually only two *new* things that the New Testament deals with, things that the Old Testament saints had never dreamed of. In fact these two things caught the Jews completely off-guard; they stumbled over these two points. In themselves they are staggering concepts, so it's no wonder that the entire New Testament is devoted to them. They are the finishing touch to God's system of salvation that was so laboriously developed in the Old Testament. The Apostles (by means of the Spirit of God) grasped the importance of these two points and how necessary they are to finish and even make possible the solution to sin and death. Without them the great Jewish system would have ground to a halt; with them, it becomes Christianity.

The point of the New Testament can be put like this:

The New Testament reveals the New Man, and how we become one with him.

God's sole aim throughout history was the restoration of man. What he wants is for us to be perfect again, as he originally designed us. And in the Old Testament he worked out a plan that will erase our past, purify our hearts, and make us fit to live with him forever. What was lacking, however, was the motive power that would make it work. The Jews, even knowing all the details about salvation, never succeeded in following all the necessary steps. Everyone failed God somewhere along the line, in some way.

So God did it himself. The ***first new thing*** that the New Testament has for us is that God became a man. The incarnation of Christ was something that the Old Testament never even hinted at, it was so unheard of. That's why the Jews reacted so violently against Jesus' statements about having come from his Father in Heaven. But it

114

was a vital step in the plan, because without it we could never be saved from sin and death. We knew that God planned to work out this problem himself from several key OT passages (for example, see Isaiah 63:6), but becoming a man was a surprise.

This New Man enters the Bible in the Gospels full of the power of the Spirit – which was the motive force that was necessary to make the Old Testament system work. Jesus obeyed the Law to the letter, to its very depths; this is something that God has wanted to see a man do since the beginning of time. Jesus loved his Father and lived solely to do his will. He loved man and worked day and night for their physical and spiritual benefit. He hated sin. He fought the enemy with the power of the Spirit and won all confrontations. He was filled with wisdom and insight. His entire life was holy – that is, set apart for God's use alone.

Nobody else could have done this like the Son of God. For thousands of years the Jews tried and failed to please God with this Law. But Jesus was different; in a single lifetime he achieved what generations of Israelites couldn't do before him. "This is my Son, whom I love; with him I am well pleased." (Matthew 3:17)

Now that a perfect life had been lived according to the high standards of God's Law, Jesus could pay the price for our sins. His death – the death of a righteous man – was the sacrifice that finally appeased the wrath of God against sinners. A substitute (which the Law allows, because of the mercy of God) took our punishment upon himself so that we might be set free from condemnation. Again, this could not have happened in the Old Testament because the animal sacrifices that were used in the Temple ceremony were only a symbol, a shadow, of what God really had in mind. Their lives weren't precious enough to God to substitute for ours.

To finish the job, God raised Jesus from the dead into eternal life, and lifted him high above all things in the universe – to his own right hand, sitting on the throne of Heaven. Now a *man* sits as co-regent with God! The resurrection of Christ wasn't just for his own sake, but was a key step in *our* salvation. It's not as if Jesus wanted to do any of this for his own benefit; he already had a perfect life with the

Father before the world was made. He became a man so that *we* might become one with God. He did this so that we might be saved.

That's the **_second thing that is new_** in the New Testament. The Old Testament continually preached the need for us to be holy, to be righteous, to live for the will of God – but it never imagined that God wanted to do something even greater than that and bring us to Heaven to be his children. To make sure we become holy and stay that way forever, God's solution is for us to be united with Christ the Holy One, his Son. We have become part of his very body, his life. Now we can't fail! Now wherever Jesus goes, we go with him; whatever he does, we do with him. He became heir of God's Kingdom and so do we who are united with him. He became the second Adam, the firstborn of a new race destined for the Throne of Heaven.

If this is our destiny, how in the world are we going to become one with Christ? It's not going to be an Eastern religion experience where spirits just melt together and become one big spiritual blob. The answer lies in the work of the Holy Spirit. He was always there in the Old Testament, just below the surface of everything that God did with his people. What nobody knew was how integral the Holy Spirit would be to our salvation. There is nothing in the Old Testament that teaches us that the Spirit of Christ is going to enter our spirits and make us one with Christ: Jesus lives in us through his Spirit, and we live in him.

This is the mystery that the Apostles revealed to the Church.

> I have been crucified with Christ and I no longer live, but Christ lives in me. The life I live in the body, I live by faith in the Son of God, who loved me and gave himself for me. (Galatians 2:20)

> I have become its servant by the commission God gave me to present to you the word of God in its fullness – the mystery that has been kept hidden for ages and generations, but is now disclosed to the saints. To them God has chosen to make known among the Gentiles the glorious riches of this mystery, which is Christ in you, the hope of glory. (Colossians 1:25-27)

Jesus longed for the day when he could bring his "sheep" together and they would have fellowship with himself and with the Father.

> I pray also for those who will believe in me through their message, that all of them may be one, Father, just as you are in me and I am in you. May they also be in us so that the world may believe that you have sent me. I have given them the glory that you gave me, that they may be one as we are one: I in them and you in me. May they be brought to complete unity to let the world know that you sent me and have loved them even as you have loved me. (John 17:20-23)

The act of making us one with Christ is a mystery indeed; nobody can understand how it works or how to make it happen. But the Creator who made the world knows how to recreate us in his image – a second Creation, not able to fall into sin and death again but able to live in the presence of God. Making the Son of God a man was the open door for humanity to live with God. The way that you and I can take advantage of this new opportunity is to become one with Christ ourselves through the Spirit.

If you think that this is a difficult concept to grasp, you're right. Even the angels long to look into this thing! And since God knew we would need help understanding the mystery of the Gospel, he gave us Apostles to explain it to us. You will also notice that they don't spend much time on the basics – they're too busy explaining the new material, which is difficult enough to understand. They assume that the reader has done his homework already in the Old Testament.

> We have much to say about this, but it is hard to explain because you are slow to learn. In fact, though by this time you ought to be teachers, you need someone to teach you the elementary truths of God's word all over again. You need milk, not solid food! Anyone who lives on milk, being still an infant, is not acquainted with the teaching about righteousness. But solid food is for

the mature, who by constant use have trained themselves to distinguish good from evil.

Therefore let us leave the elementary teachings about Christ and go on to maturity, not laying again the foundation of repentance from acts that lead to death, and of faith in God, instruction about baptisms, the laying on of hands, the resurrection of the dead, and eternal judgment. And God permitting, we will do so. (Hebrews 5:11 – 6:3)

The disciples of Jesus (who were later the Apostles – the "ones sent out") were hand-picked eyewitnesses who spent three years with Jesus. They saw his works, they listened to his lessons, they pondered over the events surrounding the life of Christ. But even they had little idea of what was happening. Until the Spirit of God filled them at Pentecost. Then the mystery was made plain to them and they had supernatural ability to carry the *right* message to the nations. They saw the truth about **the nature of Christ** and they knew the steps to take to **become one with the Son of God**. They became the teachers of the Church; we understand the true nature of Christ and his work through their teachings.

Consequently, you are no longer foreigners and aliens, but fellow citizens with God's people and members of God's household, ***built on the foundation of the apostles and prophets***, with Christ Jesus himself as the chief cornerstone. (Ephesians 2:19-20)

Since the Spirit of Christ is the key to being one with Christ, the Apostles explain difficult but critical concepts like being filled with the Spirit, and walking in the Spirit, and not grieving the Spirit.

They also teach a great deal about the New Creation. They don't want us to make the same mistake that the Jews made, thinking that the old physical system is God's ultimate goal for his people. The Epistles of the New Testament contrast the old world with the new world; they show us Heaven, and the glory of God in the Church. They press on us the need for conversion of the soul, not just outward conformity to the Law.

And speaking of the Jews, one point that the Apostles were careful to make clear is that anybody can come to Christ for salvation and the New Creation – not just the Jews. The promise was always there in the Old Testament that God would eventually extend his plan around the world; the Jews were the first to learn about it, but they are not the *only* ones allowed into God's Kingdom! It was always predicted that the Gentiles would eventually come into the family of God; but the Old Testament never fully explained how it was to happen. The reason for that is that it requires an understanding of the second mystery that the Apostles revealed to the world: that to become spiritual children of God, we must become one with Christ. In other words, it's not enough to be a Jew, but you must become a Christian – and *both* Jew and Gentile must do that to be an heir of Abraham.

The Apostles were actually interpreters of Christ. Like the Pharisees, it was entirely possible to look at Jesus of Nazareth and miss the point about him. Because he came as a man, it was easy to miss his true glory. Only by faith can we see the Son of God in Jesus and his work. But just in case we missed the point in the Gospels from Jesus' teaching, the Apostles also focus on that point in their letters. There should be no mistaking their message: the Messiah has come to gather his people to himself and take them to Heaven. The old promises that God made to his people are true; but the *way* he plans to fulfill them is completely unexpected – this time it's going to work.

Prophecy – Fulfillment

So you can see then that the Old Testament paints an almost complete picture of the salvation that God has for his people in Christ. The New Testament adds two more elements to that picture, but they are key elements that should be good news to God's people – it guarantees that the Jewish system will come to life. The Israelites struggled for a long time to make it work, but they were missing the last important key. We now have that key in the Spirit of Christ.

The sections of the Bible

The Bible can very easily be divided up into sections that follow its timeline. As the Israelites experienced what it's like to live with their God, from Egypt to Canaan to Babylon and then back to Jerusalem, the record was kept in their scrolls and remembered in sequence.

This is not to say that the Lord worked in different ways in different time periods. Though many people believe this, it's a very superficial way of looking at the Bible. Just dig a little deeper and you will see, for example, the Law from beginning to end, the Gospel from beginning to end, the Kingdom of God from beginning to end – and the New Testament uses *all* these themes for a foundation for the Christian's faith. Israel's history follows a sequence of events, but that doesn't mean that God discarded one method and moved to another one when the needs of the times changed. It simply means that he used the historical, sequential method to teach us *all* the richness and depth of his Kingdom.

For instance, we learn geography in the same way: first we learn about geography in America, then in Europe, then Asia, and so on until the course covers the whole earth. In the case of the Bible, we also learn about different aspects of our faith in sequence, but every step is as important as the others. For example, look through this list of lessons from the major stories (in historical order) of the Old Testament:

The terms of the Gospel in the Covenant

Deliverance

What it's like to live in God's perfect Kingdom

God lives among his people

The ways of the Lord

Entering the Promised Land

What happens when we don't look to God as our Lord and King

The King pulls the nation together and rules over it

Wise Kingdom subjects

A personal relationship with God

What happens when our hearts go after other gods, other loves

Judgment

Punishment and discipline

Repentance and restoration

Any of these lessons is extremely relevant and important to the Christian's faith. If you claim that the Old Testament doesn't have much to do with Christianity, which one of these points would you leave out? In fact, are any of these points better explained in the New Testament than what we are given in the Old? Jesus himself sent his hearers back to the Old Testament for these lessons:

> 'They have Moses and the Prophets; let them listen to them.' 'No, father Abraham,' he said, 'but if someone from the dead goes to them, they will repent.' He said to him, 'If they do not listen to Moses and the Prophets, they will not be convinced even if someone rises from the dead.' (Luke 16:19-21)

This means that, to fully understand the ways and works of God, we need to study the entire Bible. We can leave out no part of it unless we want a skewed picture; heresies are born from being careless about picking and choosing parts of the Bible and ignoring others. "***All*** Scripture," Paul tells us, "is God-breathed and is useful for teaching, rebuking, correcting and training in righteousness, so that the man of God may be thoroughly equipped for every good work." (2 Timothy 3:16-17) One section of the Bible isn't more important than another, or more useful; we need it all. Every part of the Bible is on the same level as the rest.

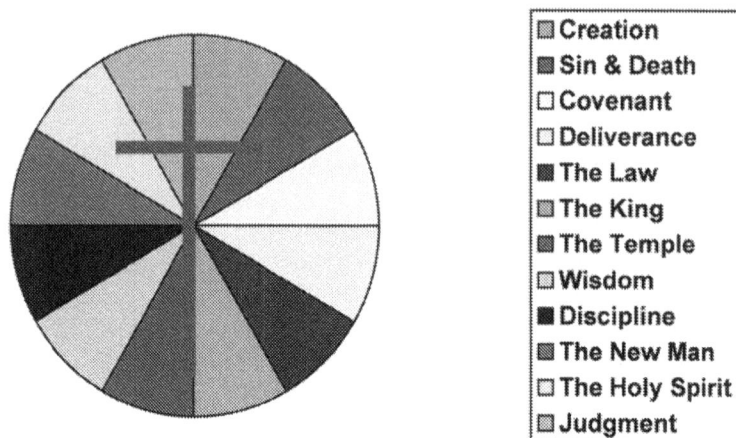

Figure 8

Every part of the Bible is an important part of the whole

Keep in mind that the point of the Old Testament is to teach us about Christ. That idea is subtle, it's underneath the surface of each story – but nevertheless real. The New Testament assures us of this. If this is how relevant the Old Testament is to Christianity, then every single lesson is extremely important for us to master!

And the point of the New Testament is to describe the New Man. This is *our* future state. As Jesus is and does, so will we be and do. So, each section of the New Testament is going to teach us how to be one with Christ so that we don't miss out on the life to come.

We will break it down like this: there are eight major sections of the Bible. We will cover each section by exploring the main ideas taught in that section, and how they are relevant for our faith. And we will explore the different books of the Bible as they form an important part of its section. By doing it this way, hopefully, you can see each book as part of the whole, as part of the story that's being told – instead of just a separate book doing its own thing.

The Sections of the Bible

The Torah – the five books of Moses (Genesis – Deuteronomy)

The Covenant of Faith and the rules of the Kingdom

The Promised Land   (Joshua – 2 Chronicles)

A land of richness and plenty, the blessings of God – and how God's people lost it

The Wisdom Literature   (Job – Song of Solomon)

How to live in God's Kingdom and have favor with God and man

The Pre-Exilic Prophets   (Isaiah – Zephaniah)

Struggling with being faithful to God – and discipline

The Post-Exilic Prophets   (Ezra – Esther, Haggai – Malachi)

Rebuilding the Temple

The Gospels and the Church   (Matthew – Acts)

The righteous life of Christ, the New Man

The Letters of the Apostles   (Romans – Jude)

Life through the Spirit of Christ

The Last Days   (Revelation)

The end of this world, and the Kingdom to come

Keys to the Bible

The Bible is a huge book, there's no denying it, and people are discouraged when they think about trying to master it. There is hope, however. In spite of the many problems, we can start getting rich treasures from the Scriptures — with some special **keys** that God has graciously made available to us. With a Bible key, a passage that used to be a hopeless mystery suddenly opens up like a treasure chest, full of useful and precious things. These aren't things "never before revealed to men" — Christians who have seriously studied the Bible in past ages have always seen them, though they didn't necessarily call them *keys* — but they may be new to you if you aren't well acquainted with the deeper things of God.

We certainly can't solve all your problems here concerning Bible study; some of them you will have to lay out before the Lord and wait on him to help you. But some of your problems may disappear when you are experienced at using the following keys to the Bible. Like opening a locked box, these principles will open up the meaning that is inside a passage that, before now, you had no idea was hidden there.

But just because you know what the keys are, that doesn't mean that you will know how to use them! A key can be a tricky thing; how does one use it? What locks will it open? Does it take a half twist or a full twist? A Bible key is much more complicated than this, of course, because we are dealing with spiritual matters that are deeper than the human mind can grasp on its own. The Spirit of God has to help us understand what we are reading, and he also has to train us in how to use the keys to the Scriptures. The whole thing is only successful if he helps us along every step.

We can use science as an example here. Back a couple of hundred years ago, scientists had little idea of the mysteries of creation because they didn't have the right tools to unlock its secrets. Only in the 20th century have they developed and used tools like electron microscopes, quantum mechanics, an understanding of DNA, and many other powerful concepts. Suddenly they are discovering so much about the world, because of these powerful tools, that they can't keep up with the new information! Our century has seen an unbelievable growth in knowledge and products that make our lives more efficient and safer because some powerful new tools in the scientist's tool kit make it all possible. They unlock the mystery of creation.

The following keys to the Bible will unlock God's Truth in the same way.[2]

- **Revelation** – The Bible is about God. That's its main purpose. The reason for this is that we can't learn the truth about God from any other source. This world shows us the handiwork of the Creator, but it reveals nothing about the love of God for his people or the wrath of God against sinners. We need God to tell us about himself. This is a mercy, because where would we be if we didn't know what God was like, what he expected of us, or what he's planning for us?

- **Miracle** – A miracle is something that God does by his own hand, apart from natural means. The reason God has to resort to miracles from time to time is because this world can't do certain things for us, naturally speaking, that we need. We're in trouble if we are only depending on this world. The hand of God alone can save us.

- **Ways** – God has ways of doing things, just as we do. He prefers working in certain ways even if we don't understand why he does it that way. His ways work; ours don't. The important thing is to learn his ways – they aren't at all like our ways of doing things – and learn to cooperate with him in this.

- **Works** – there are certain things that only God can do. We have our work to do, but some things are the special

---

[2] You can find an extended discussion of these keys in my book ***Ten Keys to the Bible***, from Ravenbrook Publishers.

domain of God. He does things that we can't do – like miracles, like enlightening the mind, like convicting the conscience, like changing a sinner into a saint. It's wise to base one's life on the works of God as on a sure foundation. Otherwise we have no hope of a future life. He is building a new Kingdom that we want to be a part of, and only what he does will last.

- **Glory** – God insists on getting the glory that is due him. The idea of "glory" is "who gets the credit?" God is behind everything that happens in this world except for one thing – our sin. He raises up nations and brings others down. He feeds all of his creatures daily. His Providence cares for us all. He builds his Church; he fights the enemy; he alone deserves the credit for building his Kingdom. But he gets almost no credit from us for any of this from sinful man! That will change, however, at the end of time, when Judgment Day reveals the hand of God guiding and shaping his Kingdom into a perfect world.

- **Faith** – Faith is a special gift that God gives us, and it makes it possible for us to live spiritually. God of course makes the first move to wake up a dead soul, but then he gives that soul the ability to see the spiritual world of God. Faith is *living in the light of God's world*. Only by faith, not by physical sense, will we see God, and his holiness, and our need of him, and the way of salvation in Christ. Without faith we are in the darkness, and we can't live as Christians.

- **Name** – the Names of God describe him. His Name sets him apart from other "gods" that people turn to. His glory is bound up in his Names: he truly is what the Name describes. We can trust him for what his Name tells us. And that is the idea behind the most important Name of God, Yahweh, the word that is behind our Bible's word "LORD." You can find the definition of this Name in Exodus 34:6-7. That description of Israel's God carries over to the name of *Jesus*, which is a combination of the word "Yahweh" with the word for "salvation." *Call on that Name* (Joel 2:32) and you will find the God you need.

- **Prophecy** – Prophecy isn't what many people think it is. It's not just predicting the future. The Prophets of the Bible were assigned a special task. In light of the way the Israelites were rebelling against God and living in immorality, the time had come to declare war against the wicked. The King himself had to come and straighten the Kingdom out, and restore justice and Law in the land. The Prophets were special ambassadors that were sent with a message: the King is coming! And he's bringing an army with him. The time has come to take God seriously and switch sides *now*, before it's too late. All the Prophets carried this message of war and the offer of mercy from the coming King.

- **Deliverance** – Actually "deliverance" and "salvation" are the same word in the original languages. And that helps us get a clear understanding of what deliverance actually is. Deliverance is *getting us out of danger and into a safe place*. It doesn't only mean that God will accept us and make us feel better, as modern "salvation" messages often tell us. If we aren't delivered out of our danger – our sin – then we aren't "saved." The Bible's examples of deliverance all show God getting his people out of trouble and putting them somewhere where they were safe from their enemy. That's our biggest spiritual need here on earth.

- **Covenant** –The covenant with Abraham is the anchor of all believers, both in the Old and New Testaments. It's actually the Gospel, as Paul tells us in Galatians 3:8. God promised to do four things for Abraham and his descendants: to give them a Son, to provide them a place to live, to make them a nation and a family, and to bless them with life. And the descendants of Abraham would all share the essential family characteristic that would insure their inheritance of the promises: his faith. (Romans 4) The Covenant with Abraham guides the entire Old Testament story as well as the New.

But just as scientific tools take some getting used to (could you work an electron microscope if nobody showed you how?) these keys to the Bible will also take some getting used to. Here are some suggestions for learning about and using Bible keys:

- ***Get used to them***. First you have to study the key itself and believe that it's true! You have to be convinced that the Bible really does teach this, that it's an important idea to learn and use.

    A Bible key is a simple yet profound idea that explains many other things in the Scriptures. But it is simple only because you master it, because you understand it so completely that you can easily apply it in any context. To be master of the key, you must do these things: **first**, find its best definition in the Bible and study it thoroughly. Somewhere there is a passage (or several) that best describes the meaning of the key. Make outlines, do word studies, find parallel passages — go through all the steps of good Bible study in order to plumb the depths of what this key is all about. Studying the keys first is time well spent: Bible study will go so much better for you in the long run if you start here first.

    Second, dwell on the key and meditate on it. To meditate on something means to go over and over it, looking at it from every angle, looking for any application of it that you can find. Believe me, the more you dwell on it and think about it, the more you will see in it; not everything comes to light during the first five minutes of reading a Bible passage! This is especially true when working with Bible keys, which are themselves critical ideas that unlock the meaning of the rest of the Bible. When you train for your life's work in school it could take years before you reach mastery of the subject. You can hardly expect less work when it comes to the divine mysteries of the Gospel and applying them to the intricacies of the human heart!

Third, don't quit working on the key until you are overwhelmed with how important it is. A Bible key isn't just an interesting way of looking at Scripture; it is essential that you use this key during Bible study or *you will not understand what you are reading.* Your salvation depends on it; God's honor is at stake; the devil and all the rest of our enemies are hoping that you *don't* see it! Thank God when it starts to dawn on you how important and powerful a principle this key is, because then the Lord is handing you the key to life and you have finally matured in your spiritual walk so that you can do something useful and honoring to God.

Fourth, understand it so well that you can tell someone else what the key is. This is more difficult than you think! They say that you are ready to teach something only when you understand at least *ten times* more about it than you intend to tell your students. That's a lot of studying! That requires a profound and deep understanding. This makes sense, of course, because it means that the teacher not only understands what the idea *means* but also knows how to *apply* it and *use* it. Have you ever had trouble finding the right words when you try to explain a difficult idea to someone else? You know what it means, but for some reason you can't seem to explain it to him. This shows that you don't understand it well enough yet. More study, more thought, more application, and eventually you will be able to explain it to anybody in clear and simple terms so that they can use the key themselves.

• ***Look for the key.*** Whenever you are reading or studying a particular passage in the Bible, keep a lookout for the key in that passage. It's there. Most people never see it, of course, because they aren't trained to see it and they don't realize the importance of the key. But Bible keys are the pillars of the Scriptures: all parts of the Word depend on them for meaning and direction.

When God wrote the Bible he used these principles as the concrete foundation and the steel girders that the rest of the building depends on. The casual observer doesn't see all that, naturally, because it is hidden by the outside "skin" that makes a first impression. But an architect knows that those foundations are there: a building can't stand without them. The trained Bible student can see evidence of the keys in every passage, giving it strength and connecting it to the rest of the Bible. In fact, nothing makes sense without the keys!

To use another analogy, a piece of furniture makes different impressions on different people. To the average buyer it is something pretty made out of wood, and it will do the job well enough. But to another craftsman it shows the skill of its maker: the joints, the square cuts, the type of finish, all show to the trained eye whether the person who made it knew what he was doing. To the average Bible reader, the Scriptures are just a collection of proof texts, verses that one can pull out of one's hat when in need that will give a pat answer to some particular problem. But to the trained student the Bible is more than that. It is a profound explanation of life, and its ideas are skillfully joined in such a way that we know that the Maker of man wrote this to instruct man in the way he should go if he wants to find life. The spiritual craftsmanship is impressive, and you don't want to miss it.

So start looking for the keys when you are reading a passage. Every passage contains at least one of the keys and probably more; unless you find them you aren't understanding the text as you ought.

• *Tie the Old and New Testaments together.* The Bible is like a large house: there are different rooms in the house, in which you do different activities; but everything is under one roof. There is not a wall between the Old and New Testaments that separates them and keeps them apart. This is one book, with common themes running all through it, though some principles may be applied in different ways in each side.

The keys are those common themes between the two sides of the Bible. You will be surprised at how well the keys explain the mysteries of both testaments. Once you understand them you will see the same ideas in the stories of early Israel as in the Church where Paul ministered. Look at it this way: the Old Testament lays out basic arguments, foundation subjects, that we need to start thinking about. It talks about God the Creator, what he had in mind with his new world, the duties of man, man's sin and how it ruins everything. And then it starts describing God's solution to man's sin so that he can get creation back on track and have something that will glorify him. The New Testament picks up on those same themes and shows the solution finally at work! It gives us the hope that this solution will result in a "new Heaven and a new earth" in the end, and God will demonstrate that he knew what he was doing all along.

The entire Bible reflects the entire kingdom of God, which after all is one single house. The statement "Moses was faithful in all God's house" (Hebrews 3:2) comes first, then it is followed with — "Christ is faithful as a son over God's house. And we are that house ..." (Hebrews 3:6) The point is that it is one house, with one builder of the house, and one family who lives in it. You can expect, therefore, that the foundation of the house (the keys) is the same for whatever room you wish to inspect.

Knowing this, you will better appreciate the Old
Testament when you go back and find the same keys
there that the New Testament depends on. This leads us
to believe that God really intended the *same things* for
those people that he has for us — though it certainly
looked different back then! This agrees with what
Scripture has to say about it: "God had planned
something better for us so that *only together with us*
would they be made perfect." (Hebrews 11:40)

- *__Go back to familiar passages with it.__* It's amazing
how these keys will open up whole new dimensions of
meaning in passages that you thought you understood
already. We may think that we understand a particular
verse because we have memorized it and used it so
much; but perhaps our understanding is still superficial,
still only skin deep. The Bible is a never-ending spring
of revelation, of new ideas and perspectives. Digging a
hole in one spot is like digging a hole in the earth: there
are thousands of miles of dirt and ore under our little
hole that we have yet to explore!

The Bible keys unlock the familiar passages just as
they do other passages. Every text stands on these
pillars of the truth, and we don't truly understand a
passage until we see its foundations and how it fits in
with the rest of the Bible. We will miss out on the real
depth of a familiar verse if we think that we have it
mastered already and we don't need to insert a key into
it as well. We may be surprised at what we will find
there!

- *__Don't let anything contradict it.__* The Bible is so
big, it deals with so many ideas, that it wouldn't be hard
to find one passage that seemingly contradicts another
passage. But the contradiction is only skin deep, so to
speak: a little more study (and sometimes a lot more
study!) will show that there is a solution to the problem.

Once you are convinced of the truth of the keys, don't let go of them. Even if you find another passage that seems to teach the opposite, don't let go of them. These keys are the *truth*, and you must see that for yourself before you can go on and understand anything else in the Bible. Sometimes it is better to let problem texts alone if you aren't ready to jump into them. You need the foundations first, the basics of the faith, before you can go on to more difficult doctrines. So if another verse causes trouble for you, you will have to wait until you get more light before you can say that you really understand it.

The Bible doesn't contradict itself, in spite of what its detractors may say about it. This book is the wisdom of God, so I'm not surprised when man has trouble understanding it. It is divine wisdom, knowledge from Heaven, God's explanations of spiritual mysteries — of course we are going to struggle through it and think that one truth seems to say the opposite of what another truth says. God is so huge, he is so far beyond man's comprehension, that we will never be able to see the *full* picture of God's nature and his ways in the way that he himself sees them. We will often have to be content with a one-sided view of things, and live with mysteries that we will never comprehend completely.

When you have problems reconciling one text with another, therefore, go with what you *know* is true and let the rest sit for a while. At least be willing to admit that you don't have infinite wisdom and you may not see all that is involved in a difficult passage! You should spend some quality time understanding the *essentials* that God expects you to master; these keys are a good place to begin.

- ***Don't get lost with secondary issues.*** The importance of the keys is to nail down what the main points of the Bible are. *These* are the things you need to be learning more about; these are what the Bible is teaching primarily. It would be a mistake, and a waste of time on your part, to be tied up with secondary issues in the text when the Bible is obviously trying to teach you about these primary issues.

For example, let's take the story about Abraham sending his servant back to Haran to find a wife for his son Isaac. Most people use this story as a lesson on finding a godly partner. Although that point is there in the story (Abraham refused to let his son marry any of the local Canaanite girls, since they were pagans) that's not the primary point of the story. Once you get familiar with the keys you will see several of them at work here: first, this is a story of **miracle** from beginning to end! It teaches the **ways** of the Lord, people living by **faith** in what they don't see but know is true, it brings **glory** to God who alone could have guided such a series of events, and it was part of the fulfillment of the **covenant to Abraham**. Limiting your study to how to go about getting married is ignoring the best parts of the story!

You should especially be careful to stick to the issues of first importance when you are starting to learn how to study the Bible. Secondary issues are just too tempting to follow, like turning aside on rabbit trails, and they don't do you nearly as much good as the primary doctrines. The human heart really is "deceitful and desperately wicked," and you will be tempted to ignore what you ought to be working on and become caught up in what will not save you. For example, I knew someone who picked up a book on the end times. She had no love for God, would never admit being a sinner, hated the things of Christ, loved the world and its ways, yet she was fascinated with the different theories on how the world is going to end! It will be little consolation for her when, at Judgment Day, she knows all about eschatology and yet loses her soul.

These are some suggestions on how to use Bible keys. Get completely familiar with them, get skilled in their use, start seeing them everywhere in the Bible, and you will find that the Word of God will become precious to you. You are going to start understanding this book that used to cause you so much confusion. You will finally become a "workman who does not need to be ashamed and who correctly handles the Word of Truth." (2 Timothy 2:15) Knowledge is power, they say, and God's knowledge is the spiritual power that builds God's kingdom. Know it well and you are going to become a powerful Christian.

The Old Testament

The History of the Old Testament

The Old Testament is a history book if it isn't anything else! On the surface it's a history of the Jews, the descendants of Abraham. On a deeper level, however, it's a history of God's special works in preparing for the Messiah – the Savior who would open up the gates of salvation and eternal life to all who will call on him, not just the Jewish race. And if you have eyes to see, as you read through the history of the Old Testament you can see the skillful steps that God takes to prepare for that great event recorded in the New Testament.

The history of the Old Testament can be broken down into eight sections.

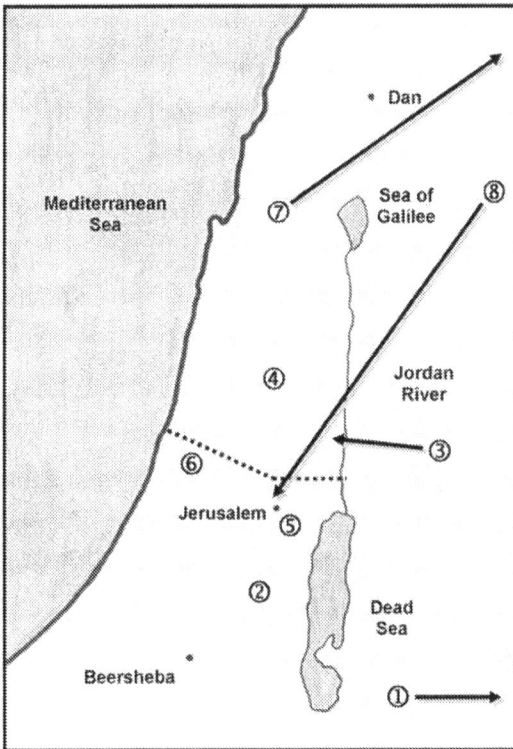

Figure 9 – Old Testament history

Map Legend:

① – *The Creation*
② – *Abraham*
③ – *Deliverance and Conquest*
④ – *Judges*
⑤ – *David and Solomon*
⑥ – *Divided Kingdom*
⑦ – *Exile*
⑧ – *Return from Exile*

From Creation to the Flood

The first history recorded tells how the world was made. It reveals that God made the world out of nothing, and it teaches us the methods that God used to create the world and everything in it. We also learn the purpose of all created things – to serve the Creator and glorify him. Man in particular is assigned the responsibility of overseeing God's Kingdom. And we will see these same methods of creation used over and over in the rest of God's works recorded in the Bible.

But we also learn why the world we have now isn't the perfect system that God created it to be – because of man's rebellion against God's Law. Because of his sin, Adam plunged the entire human race into sin and death. The whole world is suffering as a result. The problem of sin is global, infecting every civilization. God was justifiably angry at what man did to his perfect creation and, by means of the Great Flood, revealed one option for taking care of the problem: wholesale destruction. He not only has the right but the power to stop man's insanity and rebellion.

Abraham and his family

God's second option for taking care of the problem of sin is grace. He chose Abraham and made a covenant with him and his descendants forever. The covenant was a solemn promise on God's part to bless Abraham and his family with four things.

That covenant was a family treasure, passed on down through generations of heirs. It was not meant to be shared by anybody outside of the family.

Abraham lived in the land that God promised to him and his descendants – Canaan (the future Israel). His son and grandson, Isaac and Jacob, also lived in Canaan as wanderers and aliens as did Abraham.

Jacob, though undeserving and a deceiver by nature, was blessed by God in all that he did – he grew immensely rich and prosperous through God's miraculous hand. He had twelve sons, who would be the pillars of the future nation of Israel. By means of one son's rise to power in Egypt (Joseph), Jacob and his family moved and settled there to escape a wide-spread famine that struck the Middle East.

For the next four hundred years the descendants of Abraham grew to number in the millions. Unfortunately they became slaves under powerful Pharaohs and were made to work on state projects under inhuman conditions.

The Exodus and the Conquest

God heard the cries of misery of the children of Abraham suffering in Egypt, and under the leadership of Moses he broke Egypt's hold on his people and led them out of their slavery. After the miraculous crossing of the Red Sea (where the Egyptian army was destroyed), they were led to Mt. Sinai in the desert.

There they received the Law. This was the beginning of the nation of Israel. God pulled them together under one government, and the Law was the rule of God's government over them. They became his people, and he became their God. He also revealed his special name Yahweh to them and promised that they would come to learn what that name means through personal experience.

God then led them, through Moses' and his brother Aaron's leadership, through the desert to the land promised to Abraham. On the way they learned how God works on behalf of his people: through miracles. But in spite of his faithfulness in his care of them, and the miraculous power that he exercised for their benefit, they repeatedly angered him with their unbelief.

It was because they failed the test and rebelled against following the Lord into Canaan that he turned them around and sent them back into the desert to wander for the next forty years. All the adults died off (except for a faithful few). When the first generation was gone, the Lord led their children back to Canaan and, under the leadership of Joshua (Moses died at the edge of Canaan), the Israelites swept across the Jordan River. Jericho was the first pagan city to fall – and it was destroyed by means of a miracle. For the next few years the Israelites moved north and south through Palestine killing the Canaanites and taking over the land and homes for themselves. Each tribe was allotted a particular portion of the land, and finally they could settle down in peace.

The Judges

The problem was that the Israelites didn't kill off all of the Canaanites, and what God predicted would happen did happen. The surviving Canaanites led the Israelites into worship of idols and false gods. But in God's Kingdom, worship of false gods brings a swift and painful punishment. God sent various nations against Israel in war and the Israelites suffered terrible defeats, sometimes being under foreign rule for decades in abject poverty.

But when they would come to their senses and turn to the Lord for help, he would have mercy on them and send them a deliverer. These deliverers were called Judges, and usually they would raise armies to fight the foreigners. The Spirit of God obviously empowered the Judges to win the battles; the results could only be described as miraculous deliverances.

The weakness of this period of Israel's history was that the twelve tribes operated as separate political units, instead of one nation. They refused to come together under God's rule; instead they wanted to rule themselves as they saw fit. The whole situation was inherently unstable.

It wouldn't be long until the next generation would fall back into the same sins of idolatry and immorality and plunge the tribes into defeat and oppression. The cycle started all over again, and somewhere down the road God would send another Judge to deliver his people when they had had enough of suffering.

David and Solomon

The Israelites came to realize that this way of life was not acceptable. They wanted a king to draw all twelve tribes into a nation that could defend itself against its enemies.

The Lord, however, knew that even that wouldn't be good enough. Their real problem was that they were rejecting *him*. At first, however, he gave them what they wanted – the first king of Israel, Saul. In the beginning he seemed to be just the answer they were looking for: they started winning battles against the enemy, and the tribes began pulling together under him and looking to him for leadership. But soon Saul himself began rebelling against God. He was a reflection of the spiritual sickness of the whole nation, and his rule was proof that a simple political answer of a king wasn't good enough for God's people.

But David, though only a shepherd boy, was a "man after God's own heart." The Lord chose him to be king after the Israelites had lost Saul in battle. Now they would see what God wanted in a ruler: a man who would lead the people of God back to God; a man who himself bent his knee in submission to the Lord, who is the King of kings.

David immediately set about working on five necessary reforms: a capital city, defeat of the enemies of Israel, a government over all the tribes of Israel, leading the people back to God and true religion, and preparing for the building of the Temple. His agenda became the pattern that defined what God expected of all the succeeding kings of Israel; each of them were compared to their father David to see if "they had done as their father David had done."

David left a secure and strong kingdom to his son Solomon. Solomon extended the borders of the kingdom, made the nation rich and prosperous, and through his strong hand made Israel a land of peace. He also took the plans of the Temple that David had drawn up and built a house of worship for God's people. Israel reached the peak of her glory under David's and Solomon's rule.

Two Kingdoms – the Sons of David

But Solomon had enemies. The Northern tribes had never quite gotten over their misgivings of having a man from Judah, a tribe in the south, ruling over them. Under Jeroboam's leadership they rebelled against Solomon's son Rehoboam and split off to form their own nation. Thus began a split history of God's people: Israel in the north, and Judah in the south.

The trouble with Israel was that they refused to submit to David's sons (the rightful heirs of David's throne) and chose their own rulers instead. What was worse, since they would never come south to worship God in the Temple in Jerusalem, they set up golden idols in key locations in their own cities and started their own forms of worship. Baal was a favorite god of theirs. Of all their kings, Ahab (and his wife Jezebel) was the worst for the spiritual damage he did to God's people.

It was during this period that the Prophets came on the scene. Starting with Elijah, the Lord sent messengers to his people to warn them about their idolatry and immorality. Being merciful, he sent not just one but many prophets with the same message: repent now, or be destroyed when the Lord comes in his anger to tear down the idolatrous kingdom and set up a new righteous kingdom in its place. But instead of listening to the prophets, the Israelites ignored them and went on in their sin.

The end came in 722 BC. Hordes of warriors from Assyria swept through Israel, killing, burning, and carrying off captives. The custom in those days was to carry the population of a defeated nation back home and repopulate the area with foreigners – this to prevent any future rebellion. So Israel ceased to be a nation; the few Israelites left in the north ended up marrying the new foreigners and Jewish blood got mixed with Gentile blood. This was, in fact, the birth of the Samaritans – the hated breed of mixed marriages that the Jews of Jerusalem despised in the New Testament times.

Meanwhile, in the south, things weren't going much better. Judah managed to keep David's descendants on the throne in Jerusalem, but they too rebelled against God and the true worship of the Temple. Again, God sent them prophet after prophet with warnings to repent or perish. After years of rejection, God finally brought the Babylonians in 586 BC to destroy Jerusalem. The slaughter was horrific: the Temple itself was destroyed, thousands killed, thousands of others carried off into Exile to Babylon. As the prophet described it, God brought 70 years of needed rest from idolatry and immorality to the Holy Land.

The Exile

The Jews who were deported from Judah and Jerusalem actually stayed together in Babylon, unlike their brothers from the northern tribes who were scattered and lost. They learned to survive in Babylon under their new masters. In fact, they had a lot of time on their hands, and they used it profitably – they thought a lot about what went wrong back home. They saw that they angered God with their idolatry, and they went back to the Law and decided to take it more seriously.

Some of the most devout Israelites in history lived in exile in Babylon – Daniel, Shadrach, Meshak, Abednigo, Esther, and Mordechai. And God blessed them while they were in exile with leadership positions under their masters. He even protected them from disasters – for example, during Esther's lifetime the Lord kept the entire Jewish race from being wiped out by their enemies.

The Restoration from Exile

The Jews finally learned their lesson, and after 70 years in exile the Lord brought them back home to Jerusalem. Ezra, a priest who was a scholar in the Law, and Nehemiah, the governor of Jerusalem, led the people back and rebuilt the city and the Temple.

At first it was touch-and-go for the Jewish remnant. There were still enemies around who wanted to see the Jews completely destroyed. And the some of the Jews themselves put the whole project of rebuilding the land in jeopardy when they started marrying out of the faith – and bringing idolatry back into the picture. But when those problems were addressed firmly, they managed to settle down into peace and go back to the worship that Moses laid down in the Law.

The Jews became experts in the Law. They decided to take it seriously – to the letter this time. They began building up an "oral tradition" that extended the laws of Moses that would supposedly better meet the modern needs of society. But they went too far to the other extreme this time. By the time that Jesus came on the scene, the Jews (especially the Pharisees) had built up such a complex maze of man-made additions to the Law (supposedly to help them keep the Law better) that it was worthless for the needs of the soul. Their blind adherence to the letter of the Law was actually keeping them away from God. Jesus found a blind and obstinate people who could not hear the living Word of God from Heaven.

Book summaries of the Old Testament

Following is a short statement of the point of each book in the Old Testament. You realize, of course, that such a statement runs the risk of missing important lessons in the text. But sometimes it helps to get the gist of the overall book like this.

GENESIS – The beginnings of the world and God's people.

EXODUS – The deliverance of God's people into the life of obedience.

LEVITICUS – The requirements of God for his people to be holy before him.

NUMBERS – The rebellion and wanderings of the Israelites in the desert.

DEUTERONOMY – The final charges of God to his people before they enter the Promised Land.

JOSHUA – The conquest of the land of Canaan, and the possession of the Promised Land.

JUDGES – The rebellion of the Israelites in idolatry and the many deliverances that God gave them from their enemies.

RUTH – The background of the family of the future King of Israel.

1 SAMUEL – The first king of Israel – Saul – and how he compares with God's choice – David.

2 SAMUEL – The story of David and his kingdom, along with the failure of his family.

1 KINGS – The kingdom in Solomon's hands and how it split into North and South.

2 KINGS – The degeneration of both North and South (with some notable exceptions) that led to the Exile.

1 CHRONICLES – The kingdom of David and his military successes.

2 CHRONICLES – The Southern kingdom from Solomon to the Exile.

EZRA – The return of the Exiles to Jerusalem and the reinstating of the Law of God.

NEHEMIAH – The return of the Exiles to Jerusalem and the rebuilding of the walls and defenses.

ESTHER – The protection of God over the Jews during their captivity.

JOB – The story of a man's search for the meaning of suffering in God's world.

PSALMS – The songs of praise and worship that are fitting to offer to God, both corporately and privately.

PROVERBS – The wisdom necessary for living in God's world.

ECCLESIASTES – A warning against basing one's life on anything under the sun.

SONG OF SONGS – The celebration of husband and bride, the enjoyment of each other – our relationship to God.

ISAIAH – The challenge to Israel to repent, and the vision of the Heavenly Jerusalem.

JEREMIAH – The tearful agony over a country that refuses to repent of its rebellion toward God.

LAMENTATIONS – The mourning over the destruction of Jerusalem.

EZEKIEL – The Lord leaving his people and the Temple, and the Kingdom and Temple he is making plans for.

DANIEL – The plans of God for the nations throughout history, and the Messianic kingdom to come.

HOSEA – The mourning of the lover for his beloved – the Lord and his prostitute people who love other gods.

JOEL – The fierce judgment – the Day of the Lord – about to come upon the heads of the Israelites.

AMOS – The false worship and complacent pride of Israel – and God's promise to destroy and rebuild the nation.

OBADIAH – The promise of destruction to Edom for turning a deaf ear to Israel's pain.

JONAH – The story of God's mercy to *any* man who will repent.

MICAH – The fall and reinstatement of God's people.

NAHUM – The promise of destruction to Nineveh for touching the apple of God's eye.

HABAKKUK – The reasons why the Lord uses pagan unbelievers to judge his people Israel.

ZEPHANIAH – The destruction of Jerusalem and surrounding nations in the Day of the Lord, and a promise to the remnant.

HAGGAI – The warning to the returning Jews to take care of God's house.

ZECHARIAH – The future leaders of Israel – God will rule through them and redeem the people.

MALACHI – The reasons why God still doesn't think the Jews are obeying the Law.

Characters of the Old Testament

There are hundreds of people mentioned in the Old Testament; just read the genealogies to find more names than you can keep straight! But there are several characters – men, women and children – who play major roles in the story of the Old Testament. Following are some of these better known characters with a short description of their part of the story.

AARON

The first priest of Israel. He was the brother of Moses, born in Egyptian captivity, and he helped Moses lead Israel out of bondage. He had four sons, two of whom were killed by God when they refused to minister in the tabernacle by the rules of the Law. Aaron himself got into trouble several times because he yielded to the Israelites' pressure to reinstate idolatry. He died during the desert wanderings without reaching the Promised Land. (*See Exodus through Deuteronomy, and Psalm 133*)

ABEL

The second son of Adam and Eve. He offered a pleasing sacrifice to God, which made his brother Cain jealous. Cain killed Abel while they were out together in a field, and he may have tried to hide the body; but God knew about Cain's sin, and righteous Abel's blood was something God had to avenge. (*Genesis 4; Hebrews 11:4*)

ABRAHAM

The first of the Patriarchs, and the father of all the faithful. God called him to leave his family and country and go to a land that God planned to give him for an inheritance. It was to Abraham that God gave the Covenant, and from Abraham came the nation of Israel – the recipients of Abraham's Covenant. Abraham's faith in God – trusting in him despite the impossibilities – is the model for the entire Church. (*Genesis 12-25; Romans 4*)

ABSALOM

One of the sons of David, a handsome man with a winsome personality. He early showed his propensity to take matters in his own hands (avenging his sister's rape). He raised an army and threatened to wrest the kingdom from his father, but failed and was killed by accidentally hanging himself by his hair in a tree and offering a perfect target for Joab's spears. (*2 Samuel 13-18*)

ADAM

The first man, created by God from the dust of the ground. He was charged to be fruitful (which he was) and have dominion over the earth (which he did). But he didn't follow God's command about the fruit of the Tree of the Knowledge of Good and Evil – he was therefore doomed to death with all his posterity. He is the model of a natural man and how we cannot please God in our own efforts. (*Genesis 1-3; Romans 5:12-19*)

AHAB

A notoriously evil king of the northern kingdom of Israel. He and his wife Jezebel were a thorn in the side of the prophet Elijah, though he made their lives pretty miserable too. Amos turned whatever good was left in the kingdom into an idol-worshipping country and paved the way for the coming destruction from the Lord. He died in battle while disguised as a common soldier. (*1 Kings 16:29-22:40*)

AMOS

One of the prophets of Israel, the northern kingdom. He was fascinating because he was an ordinary shepherd whom the Lord called into the prophetic ministry (unlike many other prophets who had priestly backgrounds). He had no fear leveling his scathing attacks against the wicked nobility, and was famous for his line "Let justice roll on like a river, righteousness like a never-failing stream!" (*Amos*)

BALAAM

A pagan priest who lived during the Exodus period of Israel. He was hired by one of the local kings to curse Israel (which, by reason of their wanderings, was posing a threat on the local political scene). He couldn't carry out the request, however, because of God's sudden appearance and threat to him: bless them or else! His donkey, interestingly, was used by God to impress Balaam about the seriousness of harming Israel. (*Numbers 22-24*)

BATHSHEBA

The wife of Uriah the Hittite. She slept with King David and bore him a son by the adulterous act. One wonders what sort of woman she was, putting herself in public view for David to see and not objecting to the sinful relationship. She later bore David another son – Solomon – and went to great lengths to make sure he became the next king of Israel. (*2 Samuel 11-12; 1 Kings 1*)

CAIN

The first son of Adam and Eve, and the brother of Abel. His sacrifice of grain to the Lord was unacceptable – due to the fact that his lack of faith led to ignorance of what God wants in worship. He killed Abel out of jealousy; the Lord condemned him to bear the mark of history's first murderer. (*Genesis 4*)

CYRUS

The first Persian emperor of the Middle East, who defeated the Babylonians. In reviewing the historical archives of the kingdom he discovered the records of the Jews and their captivity. He gave them permission to return to Jerusalem, and provided royal protection from their enemies – thus fulfilling an old prophecy of Jeremiah. (*Jeremiah 25: 12; 29:10-14; Ezra 1*)

DANIEL

One of the best known of Israel's prophets, he was deported with thousands of other Israelites when Jerusalem was destroyed by the

Babylonians. He rose through the political system of Babylon while still holding to his devout Jewish lifestyle. He made predictions about the future of world domination which we are still seeing enacted. (*Daniel*)

DAVID

The most famous of Israel's kings. He rose from a shepherd boy to a fighter to a king, becoming the pattern for all the kings who followed him. His reign was the golden era of Israel's history. The Messiah himself was to take David's throne. David was also a leader in Israel's worship, writing many of the Psalms. (*See Samuel, Kings, and Chronicles; Psalms*)

DEBORAH

One of the judges of Israel. When Sisera formed an army and threatened the Israelites, Deborah tried to get Barak to lead the Israelites against their enemies. Barak refused, and she therefore took him and the army to the battlefield. She made a song about the victory that goaded the men about their reluctance to take on the job. (*Judges 4*)

ELI

A priest of Israel who lived during Samuel's youth, immediately before the kingship of Saul. He was too lax in running affairs at the temple, especially in not monitoring the wickedness of his sons. He died falling off his chair upon hearing the news of the Philistines capturing the Ark of the Covenant. (*1 Samuel 1-4*)

ELIJAH

A powerful prophet of the northern Kingdom. He lived during King Ahab's time and was specially assigned to address the evils of that reign. Through miracles, catastrophic confrontations with the prophets of Baal (e.g., on Mt. Carmel), and fierce denunciations against Ahab and Jezebel, Elijah made known God's opinion of the Northern kingdom's activities. God took him to Heaven in a flaming chariot. (*1 Kings 17 – 2 Kings 2*)

ELISHA

Another powerful prophet of the northern kingdom Israel. He lived with Elijah a short time, witnessed his miraculous ascent to Heaven, and inherited his cloak. He carried on the work of the Lord's war against the wickedness of Israel by means of miracles and denunciations. (*1 Kings 19:19 – 2 Kings 13*)

ENOCH

One of the earliest inhabitants of the earth, and at least the great grandfather of Noah. He evidently had a real faith in the Lord that exceeded any man of his time. The Scripture says that God came and took Enoch to Heaven before he died – one of two men of whom such a thing was recorded. (*Genesis 5:21-24; Jude 14-16*)

ESTHER

A Jewess who lived in captivity in Babylon after the destruction of Jerusalem. She was chosen to be the queen of King Xerxes. She took her life in her hands and pleaded with the king for her fellow Jews to be spared the sentence of death that the king had already signed under the deceit of Haman. (*Esther*)

EVE

The mother of the human race, the wife of the first man. Adam named her Eve because "Eve" means "living" – she was the mother of all the living. She was the first to fall into sin, being deceived by the serpent into listening to her own desires and disobeying God's command. (*Genesis 1-3; 2 Corinthians 11:3; 2 Timothy 2:11-15*)

EZEKIEL

A prophet who lived through the destruction of Jerusalem in 587 BC. He was from the priestly class and therefore knew a good deal about both the requirements of the priests and the Temple worship. He blasted the wicked priests of Jerusalem, saw the Spirit leave the Temple, and predicted the day when true worship would be reinstated in the Temple. (*Ezekiel*)

EZRA

A priest who led some of the Israelites out of their captivity in Babylon and back to Jerusalem to rebuild. He was an expert in the Law of God and took great pains to teach it to the people, making sure they understood it. He interceded for the people when they fell back into the old sins that they were punished for through the Exile. (*Ezra; Nehemiah 8*)

GIDEON

One of the judges of Israel. He was basically a nobody whom God picked to lead the Israelites against the Midianites, who were persecuting the Israelites. He chose 300 men and with them defeated the entire enemy army. He later fell into sin by making an idol for the Israelites to worship. (*Judges 6-8*)

HEZEKIAH

One of the kings of Judah, the southern kingdom. He was a breath of fresh air in the line of kings, because he feared God and made sure the kingdom did the same. During his time the king of Assyria sent Sennacherib and his army to destroy Jerusalem; Hezekiah prayed to the Lord, and the next day there were 185,000 dead Assyrians on the field. Hezekiah later feared the Assyrian king, sending him tribute, which brought a promise of trouble in the future. (*2 Kings 18 – 20; Isaiah 36-39*)

HOSEA

One of the prophets of the northern kingdom Israel. His prophecy breathes a special air of God's love for his people – he likens Israel to a wife gone to prostitution, and shows God's desire to see her come back again. The lesson was made extremely graphic for the prophet in that his own wife was a prostitute. (*Hosea*)

ISAAC

The only son of the union of Sarah and Abraham. His birth was supposed to be impossible – both his parents were old and Sarah was beyond the age of child-bearing. "Isaac means "he laughs", reflecting his parents' first reaction at the thought of having a child at their age. God later demanded that Abraham give up his son; the Lord prevented it at the last minute, satisfied that Abraham was ready to do even this in faith. (*Genesis 18: 5; 21:1-13; 22; Galatians 4:21-31*)

ISAIAH

One of the prophets of the southern kingdom Judah. He also was of the priestly class and knew the sins of his contemporaries well. His prophecies give us the clearest picture of the person and work of Christ; the Messianic sections of the book portray Christ's work to great detail. Isaiah looks beyond the judgment that is coming to the day when there will be "a new heavens and a new earth." (*Isaiah*)

JACOB

The third of the Patriarchs, the son of Isaac and brother to Esau. He was a deceiver and schemer from birth – he tricked his brother into selling his birthright, and his father into giving him the inheritance. He had 12 sons by 4 women – the beginning of the 12 tribes of Israel. He wrestled with God and won his blessing; he later followed his son Joseph into Egypt and died there in peace. (*Genesis 25:19-34; 27-30*)

JEREMIAH

One of the prophets of the southern kingdom Judah. He is also known as the "Weeping Prophet" because he lamented the state of God's people. He continually and faithfully warned them of their sin and the impending judgment, and was always in trouble with the authorities for his forthright preaching. He was abducted to Egypt with the fleeing Israelites against his will. (*Jeremiah, Lamentations*)

JEROBOAM

The first king of the northern kingdom Israel. The 10 northern tribes decided that they had taken enough rough treatment from David's ruling descendants in the South, especially since David's grandson Rehoboam proved to be stubbornly rigid with them. Jeroboam led the North into political autonomy and set up an alternative religious center in Bethel so that they wouldn't have to go to Jerusalem – thus leading them into idolatry. (*1 Kings 11:26-14:20*)

JEZEBEL

The infamous queen of Ahab, who was king of the northern kingdom Israel. She was the epitome of a worldly socialite who craved complete control over the kingdom. She especially hated Elijah and was continually trying to have him killed. She led her husband into savage acts of wickedness. Eventually she died an ignominious death and her body was eaten by dogs. (*1 Kings 16:29 – 21:29; 2 Kings 10:1-17; Revelation 2:20*)

JOAB

The general of David's army. He was bold, outspoken, and sometimes operated against David's wishes – but always with the goal of strengthening David's hand over the kingdom. He was with David from his rise to kingship until his death. At the end he conspired against Solomon becoming king, and he was cut down in the sanctuary while holding on to the horns of the altar. (*2 Samuel, 1 Kings 1-3*)

JOB

A righteous man who lived either immediately before or after the Flood (note his age at death). He was a very wealthy and influential man who lost everything he had as a test from the Lord. He knew it wasn't anything he had done, but he learned that God will do whatever pleases him; hardships and trials come to us for many reasons, not often obvious to us. (*Job*)

JONAH

One of the most famous prophets of Israel. The Lord wanted him to preach judgment to the people of the city of Nineveh, but he knew that they would repent – so he tried to escape God's call. After being swallowed by a great fish, he repented and went to do the job. Then he was disappointed to see that they all repented when they heard the Lord's message of doom. (*Jonah, Matthew 12:38-42; Luke 11:29-32*)

JONATHAN

The son of Saul (first king of Israel) and a personal friend of David. He often warned David of his father's wrath. They made a pact together that they would look out for each other's interests. Jonathan was killed in a battle with the Philistines, and David looked out for Jonathan's sons during his own reign. (*1 Samuel 18-31; 2 Samuel 1; 4; 9; 19*)

JOSHUA

The general of Israel during Moses' time and second-in-command under Moses. He was one of the spies sent into Canaan and, contrary to most of the others, encouraged them to go in and take the land. He survived the wanderings in the desert and led the tribes into Canaan, destroying Canaanites in the north and south. He helped the tribes find their portion of the land and settle in. (*Numbers, Deuteronomy, Joshua*)

JOSIAH

One of the godly kings of the southern kingdom Judah. He became king as a boy, and when one of his priests found a copy of the long-lost Law in the Temple he ordered a wholesale reform of the Temple worship and the practices of Israel. He celebrated the Passover and invited the northern tribes to participate. (*2 Kings 22,23; 2 Chronicles 34-35*)

JUDAH

One of the sons of Jacob, and head of one of the 12 tribes of Israel. His life was often pivotal in the story of the Patriarchs: he helped to sell his brother Joseph to the slave dealers; he had two sons by his own daughter-in-law; he pleaded with Joseph in Egypt to imprison himself and not Benjamin. Jacob's blessing of Judah in Genesis 49 promises a Ruler in the future – "Shiloh" – to come from Judah's line. (*Genesis 38; 44; 49:8-12*)

KORAH

One of the priests of Israel who left Egypt with Moses and Aaron. He led 250 men in rebellion against Moses' authority, saying that *all* the Israelites were holy – why did Moses therefore consider himself so special? So the Lord had Moses separate Israel from Korah and his crew and opened up the earth at their feet, swallowing all of them and their families into the ground. (*Numbers 16; Psalms 106:17; Jude 11*)

LABAN

Brother to Rebekah (Isaac's wife), grand-nephew of Abraham. He had two daughters – Leah and Rachel – for whom Jacob worked 14 years to marry. He was determined to get as much out of Jacob as he could, but Jacob's God outwitted him in the end. He finally made peace with Jacob and agreed not to bother Jacob any more. (*Genesis 24, 29-31*)

LEAH

The older daughter of Laban and the first wife of Jacob. Her father tricked Jacob and swapped Leah for Rachel on the wedding night. She knew that her husband didn't love her as much as her sister, so she worked hard at producing children for him – a sign of blessing in that culture. It was from Leah that the Messiah descended. (*Genesis 29-31*)

LOT

The nephew of Abraham, who traveled from Ur and settled in the Canaanite region with Abraham. He lived in Sodom and had a great deal of difficulty getting along there; he was finally rescued by the angels of God just before God destroyed Sodom. His daughters had sons by him. Peter declared him to be a righteous man. Oddly enough, it was through Lot's line that David – and therefore the Messiah – came. (*Genesis 13-14, 18-19; 2 Peter 2:6-8*)

MANASSEH

Probably the most wicked king of the southern kingdom Judah. Ironically he was the son of one of the most righteous kings – Hezekiah. He had a long reign and instituted idolatry, immorality, and human sacrifice throughout Israel. He did have a last minute repentance, however; but the damage was done, and the Lord was determined to punish Judah with Exile. (*2 Kings 21; 2 Chronicles 33*)

MELCHIZEDEK

A priest of the Most High God – at a time when one wouldn't have expected such a priest! It was long before the priesthood of Israel was set up. He was "King of Salem." After Abraham rescued Lot he came to Melchizedek and gave him a tenth of the spoils; Melchizedek in turn blessed Abraham. The New Testament finds in him a type of Christ, because of the nature of his priesthood. (*Genesis 14: 20; Psalm 110:4; Hebrews 7*)

MICHAL

A wife of David, daughter of Saul. David gained her in marriage for slaying Goliath. She saved David's life once. She was also taken away from him by her father and given to someone else, then restored to David. In the end she was ostracized by David for ridiculing the way he celebrated before the Lord. (*1 Samuel 18,19,25; 2 Samuel 3,6*)

MIRIAM

The sister to both Moses and Aaron, born in captivity in Egypt. When Pharaoh's daughter found Moses in the rushes, Miriam made sure that her baby brother was nursed by his own mother. She celebrated the deliverance from Egypt by making a song that became famous. When she became jealous of Moses, the Lord struck her with leprosy and healed her only on behalf of Moses' prayer for her. (*Exodus 2,15; Numbers 12*)

MORDECAI

Uncle of Esther (queen of King Xerxes), who lived during the Exile in Babylon. He refused to bow down to the king's officials, especially wicked Haman. He urged his niece to plead with the king that he would cancel his order to kill all the Jews. When the king found out Haman's plots he killed Haman instead and put Mordechai in his place as a chief official. (*Esther*)

MOSES

Probably the most famous character of the Old Testament – the Lawgiver of Israel. Born in Egypt under slavery, he turned aside from the pleasures of Pharaoh's court and sided with his fellow Hebrews. The Lord used him to lead Israel out of Egypt; through Moses the Lord gave his Law to the new nation and led them through the wilderness to the Promised Land. (*Exodus – Deuteronomy*)

NAMAAN

A Syrian general who had leprosy. He learned from one of his captive servants (an Israelite girl) that Elisha the prophet could heal him; when he went to see the prophet, Elisha told him to dip into the Jordan River 7 times to be healed. At first his pride wouldn't let him; but when his servant challenged him to do "this simple thing," he followed the prophet's orders and was healed. (*2 Kings 5*)

NAOMI

An Israelite who lost her husband and sons to death. She left her new home in Moab and returned to Israel, taking with her the widow of one of her sons – Ruth. Naomi was instrumental in getting Ruth and Boaz married. (*Ruth*)

NATHAN

A prophet of Israel, contemporary with David. He was usually the means through which the Lord spoke to David; he had no fear in confronting David about his adultery with Bathsheba. He also helped Solomon gain his throne after David's death, officiating at the ceremony. (*2 Samuel 7, 12; 1 Kings 1*)

NEBUCHADNEZZAR

The king of Babylon who conquered Jerusalem and took the Israelites into Exile. He was a famous king in general history as well as Biblical history; he built the Hanging Gardens and extended the city territory. He angered the Lord with his pride, and his mental state was reduced to that of an animal for seven years; after this, Nebuchadnezzar repented of his pride and was restored to his throne. (*2 Kings 24-25; 2 Chronicles 36; Daniel 7*)

NEHEMIAH

One of the ruling classes of the Israelites who lived in Babylon during the end of the captivity. He gained permission from King Cyrus to return to Jerusalem and rebuild the city. He had to keep the people working as well as make defenses against their watching enemies. It was due to his tireless efforts that the Jews were able to establish themselves again after the Exile. (*Nehemiah*)

NOAH

The only man in his time whom God felt was a righteous man. The Lord instructed Noah to build an ark and save himself, his family, and representatives of all the creatures on earth from the destructive Flood. The Lord made a covenant with Noah after the disaster to never destroy the earth through a flood again. All mankind is descended from Noah as well as from Adam. (*Genesis 6-9; 2 Peter 2:5*)

PHARAOH

Actually a title rather than a person, though the Bible tells us of two men specifically. The first was the king of Egypt who made Joseph his second-in-command. The second lived 400 years later, when the Lord sent Moses against him to deliver the Israelites from his cruel bondage over them. The second Pharaoh was made an object lesson, showing what happens when one resists God's commands. (*Genesis 41-50; Exodus 3-15*)

RACHEL

The younger daughter of Laban, and the one whom Jacob really wanted to marry. After being tricked into taking Leah first, Jacob worked another 7 years for Rachel. She sided with Jacob against her father and took her father's idols (giving her the right of inheritance). She was the mother of Joseph and Benjamin, and died while giving birth to her last son. (*Genesis 29-31, 35*)

REHOBOAM

The son of Solomon, grandson of David, who was king of the southern kingdom Judah. He obviously inherited little of his father's great wisdom; he angered the northern tribes and threatened them with retribution if they failed to humble themselves under his reign. They broke away and formed their own kingdom. He led Judah into idolatry and immorality. (*1 Kings 12-14; 2 Chronicles 10-12*)

RUTH

A woman from Moab – not a true Israelite – who married into one of the Israelite families. When her husband died, her mother-in-law was instrumental in getting her introduced to, and later married to, Boaz. Ruth was the great grandmother of King David. (*Ruth*)

SAMSON

One of the greatest Judges of Israel. He was set apart from his birth as a Nazirite – no wine, no razor on his head. The Spirit of God used Samson to perform remarkable feats of strength against the Philistines. In frustration his enemies used Delilah to find out the secret of his strength, and they overpowered him at last. But the Lord restored his strength for one last act of deliverance. (*Judges 13-16*)

SAMUEL

The last of the Judges of Israel. His birth was miraculous, and his childhood was devoted to the service of the Lord under Eli's priesthood. The Lord used Samuel to choose the first king of Israel – Saul. He also used him to take away the kingship from Saul and give it to David, one of the sons of Jesse. (*1 Samuel*)

SARAH

The wife of Abraham who came with him from Ur to Canaan. She was also his half sister, born of the same father but not of the same mother. Thus Abraham passed her off twice as his sister out of fear of the kings of the land he lived in (Pharaoh in Egypt and Abimelek in Canaan). She laughed when the angel of God predicted she would have a son in her old age. (*Genesis 12-23; 1 Peter 3:6*)

SAUL

The first king of Israel, from the tribe of Benjamin. Samuel picked him to be king; he was a tall man and a natural leader. He became extremely jealous of David's rising popularity and spent most of his reign trying to hunt David down and kill him. He angered the Lord by offering up a sacrifice with his own hands, and the Lord took the kingdom from him. He died in battle with the Philistines. (*1 Samuel*)

SOLOMON

The son of David and Bathsheba, to whom the Lord gave an uncommon wisdom in answer to his prayer. By the time he became king, the kingdom was established and their enemies were subdued. He built the Temple (thus making obsolete the Tabernacle), huge palaces for himself and his many wives, wrote books of wisdom, and got himself into trouble near the end of his life through his wives' idolatry. (*2 Samuel 12:24-25; 1 Kings 1-11; 2 Chronicles 1-9; Proverbs; Ecclesiastes; Song of Songs; Matthew 6:29*)

ZEDEKIAH

The last king of the southern tribe Judah. Nebuchadnezzar made Zedekiah king in hopes of stabilizing the situation in Jerusalem; but Zedekiah rebelled against his master and sought an alliance with Egypt. Jeremiah warned him to submit to the Lord – to cooperate with Nebuchadnezzar – but he had Jeremiah imprisoned. When the end came, the Babylonians killed his sons and put out his eyes. He was brought to Babylon with the other captives and given a place at the king's table. (*2 Kings 24-25; 2 Chronicles 36; Jeremiah 21, 24, 32, 34, 37, 38-39, 52*)

Wrong notions of the Old Testament

The Old Testament is a confusing book, and no less to the Christians. Admittedly it's huge, and it consists of hundreds of stories bound together over a tapestry of time extending from Creation to the days of the Apostles. One could get lost if he doesn't know the lay of the land.

But it's not as if God hasn't given us plenty of help to understand his own book! Jesus was frustrated, remember, with the Jews of his day, because they were deliberately distorting the plain and simple truth in the Bible – and being the scholars that they were, they should have known better.

We've already looked at how people make the Old Testament equivalent with the Law itself, so that they can write it all off and focus on grace instead of the Law. That's not being fair to the book. The Law *is* given in the Old Testament, and, yes, the Israelites were required to keep the Law to be considered righteous. But the Old Testament is bigger than the Law. Abraham came before the Law (Paul reminds us in Romans 4), and the over-all story of the Old Testament includes the Law *and* grace. The Law was *added* (Galatians 3:19) to the Covenant because sinners had to become righteous before they were allowed into God's presence. And God showed us in the Old Testament why following the Law will never work for sinners: we can't follow all of his Law. A new method (in Christ), devised from the beginning of the world, will save us from our sin in a way that the Law can't. If you don't see this bigger picture in the Old Testament, you don't truly understand it.

Here are a few other mistakes that people make with the Old Testament.

- **Allegories** – This approach was made famous by an early church father, Origen. He didn't see much use for the

166

physical aspect of the Old Testament; all that was for the Jews, not for Christians, in his opinion. But he didn't want to write off God's Word either. So he devised a system where each story represented a spiritual reality. And that, to Origen, was the only meaning that we need concern ourselves with.

The American Heritage dictionary defines "allegory" as "The representation of abstract ideas or principles by characters, figures, or events in narrative, dramatic, or pictorial form." And actually there *are* allegories in the Old Testament – Paul, for example, tells us about one in Galatians. He sees that Hagar represents the present-day Jews in their slavery to sin and death, and Sarah represents the Christian church in its freedom in Christ.

> These things may be taken figuratively, for the women represent two covenants. One covenant is from Mount Sinai and bears children who are to be slaves: This is Hagar. Now Hagar stands for Mount Sinai in Arabia and corresponds to the present city of Jerusalem, because she is in slavery with her children. But the Jerusalem that is above is free, and she is our mother. (Galatians 4:24-26)

The problem with allegories is that, once someone gets enamoured with this clever way of interpreting the text, he starts seeing allegories everywhere when they really aren't there. He starts forcing unnatural meanings on ordinary people and places.

The Old Testament is hard enough to understand without turning every story and character into a spiritual allegory. We know that we're going too far when there's no good Scriptural reason for making one point correspond to another. When we come up with fanciful ideas that we can't prove from the Bible itself, when willy-nilly anything can get substituted for another, then it's time to quit.

The first meaning of the text is the obvious, physical meaning – the meaning that the characters in the story itself would get out of what was happening to them. And Origen was wrong: if it was important to the Jews to which it happened, then what happened to them is important to us too, just as it happened. For example, a foundation stone of our Christian faith is the fact that God delivered the Jews from Egypt and slavery. There's no need to change that story to suit our spiritual tastes before it becomes important.

Next, we can look for a spiritual meaning to the story *only if the rest of the Bible encourages us to do so.* For example, we *are* told that the Exodus story has a wider meaning. First, Jesus himself was "brought out of Egypt," a point that Matthew was careful to make. (Matthew 2:15) Second, it corresponds to *our* spiritual escape from sin and death: the Passover Meal, instituted at the Exodus when Israel left Egypt, is the very basis of our Lord's Supper ceremony.

Finally, let's remember that the Apostles had a deeper revelation of Christ and his Word than we will ever get. We depend on their leading; they are the foundation of the church and guide our thoughts. They set the doctrine for Christianity.

> Consequently, you are no longer foreigners and aliens, but fellow citizens with God's people and members of God's household, ***built on the foundation of the Apostles and Prophets***, with Christ Jesus himself as the chief cornerstone. (Ephesians 2:19-20)

So when Paul says that a certain story is an allegory, we take his word for it; he knows what he's talking about. But we don't have the insight that Paul had! It's dangerous for us to run ahead of the Apostle and claim that we see extra meanings in the text that he doesn't talk about himself. It's better to let the Apostles guide us and lead us, and not run ahead of them.

- **New Testament Christians** – There are churches today that boast of being "New Testament Christians." They ought to be ashamed of themselves. Nowhere in the Bible has God told us that he has set aside the Old Testament. Yet they think that they are impressing us, and no doubt God himself, by firmly standing on the Gospel of Christ as the New Testament has it.

  They seem to have little awareness of the fact that the New Testament stands on the Old like the top two stories of a hundred-story skyscraper! You can ignore the Old Testament if you like, but careful Bible students can see its foundation there in the New, even if you can't. Jesus used it, the Apostles used it constantly as the main source in their preaching, and there are many Christians who haven't made that gross error of setting it aside.

  I think we've made our point in this book about how fundamental the Old Testament is to our faith. We learn 95% of our Christian doctrine from it. For someone to claim that they are a "New Testament Christian" is like a doctor claiming that he only went to the last year of medical school! Who would entrust himself to the care of such an ignorant "doctor"?

- **Cultic Israelite belief** – There are two ways to approach the Bible: either you believe that it's the Word of God, or you believe that it isn't. If you think that it's God's Word, then you're not really worried about *how* it came to be, because you know that Jesus uses a few loaves and fish to feed thousands; the earthly is infused with the power of Heaven to accomplish miracles – things that this world couldn't do on its own. But if you *don't* think that the Bible is God's Word, then obviously – at least it's obvious to you! – God is going to need some help from man in putting together his religion.

If you haven't heard this one, you need to be aware that a lot of people (scholars particularly) think that Judaism was a man-made religion, a composite or mix of many Eastern religions that slowly evolved in the minds of men and nations. It started with polytheism (the belief in many gods) and changed into monotheism (the belief in one God) as cultures and history shaped it. And (as the story goes) the Jews, being the religious geniuses that they were, were largely responsible for this shaping of religion from a childish, head-knocking, primitive materialism to a mature religion that we now have in the Old Testament.

Nonsense. If the Jews were religious geniuses who reshaped religion into something useable for the rest of us, why doesn't the Old Testament say so? Instead the Bible gives us a shocking judgment on the immorality and ignorance of the Jews. They were resistant to the news about the true God; they clung to the pagan gods of the cultures around them just as desperately as any Babylonian did! God forced himself into the Jewish mind, with unwelcome news – that he was not like those other religions at all. The difference between paganism and the God of the Old Testament was like night and day; it wasn't an evolutionary growth. And the Jews fought against this God all along the way.

The Bible's own account of the matter is starkly different from what these unbelieving scholars have come up with. Of course they have an ulterior motive: if they can show that man created this story about God, then we don't have to take it so seriously. And that, naturally, leads to the next point – that God's Law in the Old Testament is also man-made and can be changed to suit our own changing culture. In other words, they want a Biblical basis to sin against God.

Nowhere in the Bible will you find anything at all to support all of this. On the contrary, God clearly reveals the opposite – that he is above this world, not a part of it nor an evolutionary step of what's in it. He reveals truth to us that we couldn't have known or figured out on our own. He calls us out of this world, because this world is an immoral and broken disaster. He has always taught this, from Genesis to Revelation, and he's not going to change his story now to suit our modern tastes. And the reason that this message has always been the same, and the reason we will never find a basis for this unbelieving theory in the Bible itself, is because God knows what we will do with a little bit of wiggle room. He can't trust us.

- **Jewish only** – The Jews lived a special life under God. As Paul puts it –

> Theirs is the adoption as sons; theirs the divine glory, the covenants, the receiving of the Law, the temple worship and the promises. Theirs are the patriarchs, and from them is traced the human ancestry of Christ, who is God over all, forever praised! Amen. (Romans 9:4-5)

Unfortunately Christians don't understand the deeper level at which God was working with the Jews. Many scholars think it's unfair to impose our Christian message on the Old Testament. God, they say, was doing a special thing with the Jews, something he doesn't do with anybody else. The Old Testament is *their* Book, with God's special message to them. We Christians are no more than interested bystanders. Jesus is treating us differently and has a different agenda for us.

But that, again, ignores what the Bible says about it. God was interested primarily in their *souls*, just as he is with us.

> These were all commended for their faith, yet none of them received what had been promised. God had planned something better for us so that

only together with us would they be made perfect. (Hebrews 11:39-40)

This passage clearly ties the Old Testament Jews to the fate of the Church. The Jews were supposed to learn the lessons of Christ, just as we have them. To focus the Old Testament so narrowly that we think what God did there was *only* for the Jews is not only short-sighted, it's ripping away the foundation of Christian doctrine. God didn't work among the Jews only for them; he did it for all of his people, Jew and Gentile alike.

For example, Paul taught us that the difference between Jew and Gentile is not so great as we might have thought; the line disappears in Christ.

> His purpose was to create in himself one new man out of the two, thus making peace, and in this one body to reconcile both of them to God through the cross, by which he put to death their hostility. He came and preached peace to you who were far away and peace to those who were near. For through him we both have access to the Father by one Spirit. Consequently, you are no longer foreigners and aliens, but fellow citizens with God's people and members of God's household, built on the foundation of the Apostles and Prophets, with Christ Jesus himself as the chief cornerstone. (Ephesians 2:15-20)

In other words, Old or New Testament, Jew or Gentile, God's people share the same Word, the same salvation, the same Temple and access to the same God. It's the same story for all of us.

- **Progressive revelation** – This is a theory of the Old Testament that scholars devised in an effort to give the book at least some semblance of a Christian message. It's a subtle idea, seemingly sound, but it contains a basic flaw.

According to the theory, our Christian faith consists primarily of several key events: the incarnation of Christ, the death of Christ, his resurrection, our faith in him, deliverance from our sin, and uniting with him in Heaven. And we learned these events, of course, in the New Testament – it's there that the essential facts of Christ shine brilliantly. We use the stories that teach these events in evangelistic services to bring more people to Christ; we use the Letters of the Apostles in Sunday School lessons and Bible studies to better explain our faith to our students. The New Testament aims right at the root issue – the necessary elements of true salvation in Christ.

On the other hand (according to the theory), the Jews only had shadows to work with. Since Jesus had not yet come, they knew God only in a limited way. They were expected to live up to what they did know, but the elements of their faith consisted in the Temple, animal sacrifices, the land of Canaan – hardly a comparison to the richness of the Christian faith. That makes the Old Testament, then, a book of limited use to Christians. It didn't save the soul – or even adequately illuminate the mind – of the Israelite, so a Christian has to be careful of relying too much on a Jewish book.

It's not as if the Old Testament were perfectly useless to us, though. There is a thread of eternal truth weaving in and out of the stories that we Christians can detect. The theory is this: at the beginning of the Old Testament, particularly with Genesis 3, we are shown a faint glimpse of things to come. When God pronounced Satan's doom, he predicted the time when the woman's "offspring" would come and "crush your head" – perhaps a reference to Christ. This was the beginning of what Bible scholars have called the "scarlet thread" running throughout the Old Testament and culminating in the New Testament account of Christ.

As the Old Testament progresses, each story adds a little more to the picture of the process of salvation. Or should we say that the picture grows clearer as time goes on. We could illustrate it in this way:

| Abraham | Moses | David | Prophets | Christ |

Figure 10 – Progressive Revelation

The stories of Abraham, Moses and Mt. Sinai, Joshua and the conquest of Canaan, the Judges, David and his descendants, and the Prophets all help to bring the picture into sharper focus. But obviously we can't stop anywhere along the way and claim that we have a true idea of what we need for our Christian faith.

In other words, we are given little bits and pieces to the secret of salvation through Christ all through the Old Testament. An observant Jew would have been collecting these pieces over the ages, and could have guessed that it was leading up to something in the future, though he wouldn't know exactly what. It's always been a question as to how much the Israelites knew about the process of salvation. Could they be saved? Did their limited knowledge and limited access to God do anything for their eternal souls? At the very least, however, the careful Jew should have been willing to listen to Christ when the Lord came, though he would not have understood what his own Scriptures well enough to be saved himself.

That's the theory of Progressive Revelation. On the surface it seems to fit the facts. But when one probes a bit deeper, there are some disturbing realities that the theory doesn't fit. We don't have time to unpack the whole thing, but let's look at one of my favorite stories that will prove that this theory of a "gradually clearing" picture is the wrong way to look at it. [3]

Let's take the example of Sacrifice. In Genesis 4, with the story of Abel and Cain, we learn what the four essentials of an acceptable sacrifice are – the kind of sacrifice that God is pleased with. Here are the four elements:

- A substitute victim
- The firstborn
- Death of the victim – shedding of blood
- Atonement – acceptance from God

The significance of this story is that Abel knew what God required in a sacrifice. His brother Cain brought the wrong kind of sacrifice; through faith, however, Abel brought the kind of sacrifice that met God's requirements for the forgiveness of sin. This was long before the Mosaic Code specified the kind of sacrifice that would take away the Israelites' sins!

> In fact, the Law requires that nearly everything be cleansed with blood, and without the shedding of blood there is no forgiveness. (Hebrews 9:22)

There is only one way that Abel would have known about the expectations of God – and Hebrews tells us.

> By faith Abel offered God a better sacrifice than Cain did. By *faith* he was commended as a righteous man, when God spoke well of his offerings. And by faith *he still speaks*, even though he is dead. (Hebrews 11:4)

---

[3] You can get a full discussion on this subject in my book *A New Model for Biblical Studies* from Ravenbrook Publishers.

It's very questionable whether Adam and Eve knew about true sacrifice from God's perspective; if they had, both sons would have therefore known and Cain wouldn't have offered an unacceptable sacrifice. So Abel was given "inside information" through his faith to enable him to approach God in the right way. What this shows is that even the simplest faith, even the faith of any of the Old Testament saints, will see the same truth in God that we see.

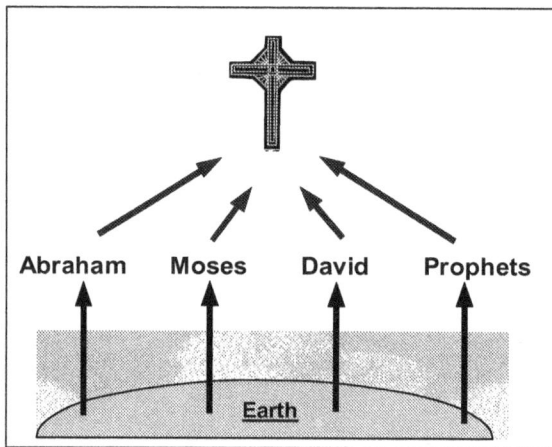

Figure 11 – Faith sees the eternal Christ

Faith dwells in eternal dwellings, not in the shadow land of the historical process.

Notice that the rest of the Bible uses these same four points whenever it discusses an acceptable sacrifice to God. There are many other kinds of sacrifices and offerings, for different purposes, mentioned in Scripture; but the fundamental sacrifice that atones for our sins and reconciles us to God is patterned after this story of Abel. The sacrificial system in the Mosaic Law is firmly based on these four principles. The sacrifice of Christ is nothing other than this pattern from Genesis 4 which Abel first learned.

Nothing in the basic structure of an acceptable sacrifice has changed over thousands of years of Biblical history and theology! So Abel still teaches us ("he still speaks") what the essentials of an atoning sacrifice are.

So, it's wrong to look at the Old Testament stories as unclear, confusing, and unusable for Christians. Rather, each story in itself is a clear, complete description of some aspect of the person and work of Christ – perfectly usable to both Jew and Christian. That means that the Old Testament isn't a book to be set aside, but a book of Christian doctrine that we need to study. The New Testament teaches us to do this.

* **Dispensations** – We have to say something about the theory of dispensationalism here, since so many people divide up the Old Testament in that way.

Basically dispensationalism teaches that the Bible divides up history into different eras in which God worked with people in different ways – supposedly their spiritual needs were different in each age. That's the nice way to put it. The fact is that the dispensationalists think that God switched methods over time because things weren't working out, and he had to come up with some other method that *would* work. To me, that makes it look as if God doesn't know what he's doing!

What that does to the Bible is to chop it up into useless pieces that we Christians can't use. The theory goes that, since God used the Law with the Israelites, and he changed methods when he went to the Gospels, that makes the Old Testament of no concern to us; it's not written for us but for the Jews. Dispensationalism also claims that the Gospels weren't written for Christians either! The only part of the Bible that directly applies to us, according to them, are the Apostolic letters since they were written to "New Testament churches."

As they "rightly divide" [4] the Bible in this way, they are conveniently ignoring what the Bible says about itself. Nor are they seeing the depth of the Bible's message. We've already seen that the bigger story of the Bible, throughout the Old as well as the New, includes Law *and* Grace. Both are vital for true Christianity. Nor do we find the Bible supporting the idea that God treated the Old Testament saints in a fundamentally different way than he does for us Christians. They were saved through faith in Christ as well as we. Besides, if it's true that our Christian doctrines are first described, and often best described, in the Old Testament, that puts the lie to the idea that God wants us to focus only on the Apostles' letters!

• **The Liberals' views** – Liberals, if you haven't run across them before now, are "Christians" who don't believe the Bible. Since most churches, and almost all Bible schools and seminaries, are infected with Liberalism, we will describe it in detail.

For the last two hundred years at least, there's been a determined attack against the Bible. Modern man has discovered, through science in particular, a new freedom and power over his world that the ancients never enjoyed. So why fear the "gods" of the world when you can run the world yourself? And the Bible is a thorn in their side, because it represents the "old" standard that "naïve" people of the past believed. It certainly doesn't allow a free lifestyle that our modern world makes so easy. So to remove the thorn, "experts" have been busy destroying the foundations of the Bible so that now only "ignorant" people would take it at face value.

Liberalism (which is the formal name for the wave of unbelief that has swept the Western world in the last two

---

[4] The KJV translation of 2 Timothy 2:15, a verse made famous by C. I. Scofield, the "founding father" of Dispensationalism.

centuries) is a way, or method, of looking at the Bible – basically, it doesn't believe it. Liberals (in some circles known as "moderates") want to keep the name Christian, but they don't want the doctrine of Christianity. It's amazing what they don't believe! They have more in common with pagan religions than the faith that the Apostles once taught.

Liberals don't believe in –

• *Miracles* – They don't believe in anything supernatural – the miracles of Christ, the miracles that Moses did in the wilderness (starting with the plagues in Egypt and the parting of the Red Sea), the miracles that the Apostles did, the miracles that the Prophets did. They especially don't believe in the very first miracle in the Bible, the biggest one of them all – the Creation!

• *Blood atonement* – The Liberals don't believe that the blood of any person or of any animal can cleanse our hearts of sin. Since the Old Testament sacrificial system depended on the blood sacrifice of animals to reconcile God and man, they claim that the whole bloody system was a carry-over from pagan religions. They are particularly offended at the thought that Jesus' death was demanded by God, and that it would bring God and man together in reconciliation, and that his blood was necessary to "cover over" (which is what the word "atonement" means in Hebrew) our sinful hearts. And of course the reason they don't believe in blood atonement is because they don't believe that man has done anything serious enough to warrant someone's death as punishment.

• *Prophecy* – Since Liberals don't believe in the supernatural, they can't believe that the prophets actually predicted events before they happened. So by their account, the Prophets wrote their "predictions" after the events happened (which explains why they were so accurate!) and then claimed to have written them before the events – sort of a pious fraud for the benefit of God's people.

• *Original authorship* – The Liberals don't believe that Moses wrote the first five books of Moses, they don't believe that Isaiah wrote Isaiah, they don't believe that Daniel wrote Daniel, (that is, they claim that the prophecies that Daniel supposedly uttered were put into his mouth by editors centuries later), they don't believe that Matthew wrote Matthew, they don't believe that Paul wrote most of the letters ascribed to him, and they have problems with many of the other books in the Bible. The reason is that they don't want to give *any credence at all* to what the Bible says about itself, not even to who actually wrote the books.

• *The integrity of the Gospels* – For over three hundred years the Liberals have been trying to destroy the story of Jesus. Their claim is that the Church, or the Apostles, turned the simple morality teachings of Jesus the Jew into a new religion that made him God. Supposedly the Gospel accounts are actually fictitious myths of the early Church; we can't really know what Jesus was really like.

• *The integrity of the original manuscripts* – There are whole sciences devoted to the study of the original documents of the Bible (they are known as "form criticism" and "textual criticism"), and their goal is to show how undependable the Bible is. Not only do they "prove" that the Bibles we have now are simply corrupted and unreliable copies of whatever the originals may have been (since nobody can know what they were like!), they also demonstrate that the Israelites and the Church borrowed very heavily from their cultures to form the Bible. In other words, just as we would use a saying from Shakespeare to make a point in our sermons, the Biblical writers used common themes and ideas in their day to form their new religion. So, the Liberals tell us, it was *not* revelation from another world. The pagan world already had these ideas worked out, and the Bible writers collected them together to form both Judaism and Christianity. Sort of like a religious plagiarism.

• *The Bible as the Word of God* – With all these problems, the Liberals have come to the conclusion that the Bible can't be the Word of God. It's obviously a work of man, full of problems, contradictions and myths. The Old Testament in particular is an immature religious work of the Jews; interesting, but not very helpful for modern man except for some morality lessons. The New Testament contains outright falsehoods from a Church anxious to lift their new "God" to divine status among the world's pantheon of gods. Just the embarrassing situation of thousands of manuscripts rarely agreeing about how the text reads should prove to anybody that the Bible is not a perfect work from Heaven!

Why would the Liberals bother to study the Bible, then, if they don't believe most of it? *First*, it gives them the aura of authority they need for their own agenda. They can claim to be teaching the Bible, get unsuspecting students to sit at their feet, and then give them everything *but* the Bible. These Bible "scholars" spend more time destroying people's faith in the Bible than they do teaching its precepts, yet they are held in high esteem by the Church and society. They genuinely think that they are doing a service to God! (See John 16:2) Their degrees and positions in Christian circles open many doors for them;

they dominate educational institutions; they dictate and direct the agenda of the Church in modern society. But they are impostors, wolves in sheep's clothing.

For certain men whose condemnation was written about long ago have secretly slipped in among you. They are godless men, who change the grace of our God into a license for immorality and deny Jesus Christ our only Sovereign and Lord . . . In the very same way, these dreamers pollute their own bodies, reject authority and slander celestial beings. Yet these men speak abusively against whatever they do not understand; and what things they do understand by instinct, like unreasoning animals – these are the very things that destroy them . . . Woe to them! They have taken the way of Cain; they have rushed for profit into Balaam's error; they have been destroyed in Korah's rebellion. These men are blemishes at your love feasts, eating with you without the slightest qualm – shepherds who feed only themselves. They are clouds without rain, blown along by the wind; autumn trees, without fruit and uprooted – twice dead. They are wild waves of the sea, foaming up their shame; wandering stars, for whom blackest darkness has been reserved forever. (Jude 4,8,10-13)

Second, it pays the bills. There's a lot of money to be made in the service of the Church. Would people actually be dishonest and use the Bible and the Church as a vehicle to material gain? Absolutely! If they jumped to another religion they wouldn't have the opportunities they have under the Church's umbrella. Life is good if you can stay in the Church, come up with your own doctrines, enjoy the fruits of immorality, and get paid for it too! Paul knew about these kinds of parasites in the Church.

If anyone teaches false doctrines and does not agree to the sound instruction of our Lord Jesus Christ and to godly teaching, he is conceited and understands nothing. He has an unhealthy interest in controversies and quarrels about words that result in envy, strife, malicious talk, evil suspicions and constant friction between men of corrupt mind, who have been robbed of the truth and who think that godliness is a means to financial gain. (1 Timothy 6:3-5)

The Liberal agenda is actually to create a new God for people to believe in, and they have given us a chopped-up Bible that includes only a few pious devotions that they are comfortable promoting. This God of theirs will allow them to do what the ancients called sin and wickedness:

Do you not know that the wicked will not inherit the kingdom of God? Do not be deceived: Neither the sexually immoral nor idolaters nor adulterers nor male prostitutes nor homosexual offenders nor thieves nor the greedy nor drunkards nor slanderers nor swindlers will inherit the kingdom of God. (1 Corinthians 6:9-10)

That list pretty much describes what many of our modern churches (and the government has followed their lead and legalized a lot of it) allow and even promote. They are after state-sponsored, church-sanctioned immorality. So the goal is to thoroughly discredit the Bible as revelation from God.

Where there is no revelation, the people cast off restraint; but blessed is he who keeps the Law. (Proverbs 29:18)

Liberal theology actually gives a great deal of relief to someone looking for a way out of the strict requirements of the Kingdom of God. If they can show that the Bible is a work of man, and basically undependable (to some degree or another – not all of them draw the lines in the same places), then its opinions aren't any better than yours or mine. If they can prove that the Bible is contradictory and imperfect, then that means we don't have to take it so seriously. What God said about right and wrong in Moses' day just may be a cultural thing and totally inappropriate for our day. If they can easily explain away the integrity and authority of the Bible (even for such a simple thing as who wrote the books!), then we are free to question everything in it – especially the parts where God makes uncomfortable demands on us! And isn't that the case? Even those people who say they believe the Bible end up contradicting each other with different views, so that everyone is confused and the Bible doesn't seem to be a real help for anybody – so obviously (the unbelievers tell us) people are taking an imperfect book way too seriously.

In the days of the early Church, such rank unbelievers would be shown to the door – and branded as heretics so that others in the community would know to stay away from them. In our day that's considered impolite behavior, so we let them stay and corrupt the minds of our youth with their poison. Now it's rare to find a church, and almost impossible to find a school, that hasn't been infected to some degree or another with Liberalism.

As to the things they deny, we've already looked at many things about the Bible that would challenge their claims. Let's look now at the fundamental problems of Liberalism, or unbelief in general.

First, they weren't there. So how can they arrogantly declare that the events in the Bible didn't happen as described there? How can a person in the twenty-first century claim that a man in Jesus' day lied in his account of the resurrection of Lazarus? John was there; the modern critic was not. No amount of theory can dismiss an eyewitness account. Such a foolish argument would be immediately shut down in a court of law as inadmissible.[5] If unbelievers want me to accept their watered-down version of the stories in the Bible, they're going to have to come up with reliable witnesses of their own who can show me, without any doubt, that the Bible writers were **lying**.

Second, their agenda is unacceptable. Unbelievers want to be free of the moral restraints of the Bible – that's why they're trying to destroy its authority. They want to be free to live immoral lives with a clear conscience. Of course they don't say that in their books, or in public; but watch them in everyday life and you will see that this is what they are after. It's sin that they love, and the Bible condemns sinners.[6] So, out with the Bible!

Third, they are being completely dishonest. If they really want to throw out most of the Bible, the least they could do is drop the name "Christian" and form some new pagan religion. They're causing a great deal of confusion in the Church by hiding under the Church's umbrella of protection and financial security. Young people in particular are susceptible to authority, and they usually don't have the discernment they need to spot a clever liar and cheat. Yet they're being indoctrinated with the Liberal's brand of "Christianity" and losing their souls in the process. Jesus' condemnation of the Pharisees leading new converts into their wickedness comes to mind here. (Matthew 23:15)

Fourth, it doesn't work. As much as the Liberals fight against the Bible and try to talk people out of it,

---

[5] In the early nineteenth century Simon Greenleaf, a professor of Law, co-creator of Harvard's law program, and trial lawyer himself, wrote an analysis of the Gospels in light of a court case. He found that the Gospels were so well presented that no critic could bring a successful case against them. *The Testimony of the Evangelists*, Simon Greenleaf; Kregel: Grand Rapids.

[6] In a private letter, Thomas Huxley ("Darwin's bulldog") admitted that one of the reasons he fought so hard for the theory of evolution is so that people would have the freedom to indulge in sexual immorality. A perfect fulfillment of Ephesians 4:18-19!

the Spirit of God overrules and convinces the child of God that it really is the Word of God. Fortunately God is bigger than man is, and when he wants someone to believe the truth, no amount of lies and strategy is going to prevail against the Spirit of Truth. Most people will fall for the lie; but the children know bread when they see it!

When the Gentiles heard this, they were glad and honored the Word of the Lord; and all who were appointed for eternal life believed. (Acts 13:48)

So unbelief is neither honest nor wise. There's too much about the Bible to casually dismiss; you need to provide legitimate evidence and testimony to successfully denounce it – certainly not mere opinions! Besides, the reason people want to belittle the Bible is to get more freedom to live in sin and ignore God's plain directives for life, though they're not honest enough to admit it.

Unbelievers often are the ones demanding "proof" for the things of God. The Pharisees in Jesus' day were the ones who caused problems in his ministry; they had no intention of believing anything he said – they just wanted a pretext for getting rid of him. But God will not cater to unbelief; he doesn't owe unbelievers a thing! He is the King, and he demands *obedience*. He is not pleased with a rebellious subject! Such behavior may get an immediate and furious response from the throne.

A king delights in a wise servant, but a shameful servant incurs his wrath. (Proverbs 14:35)

It seems that when people read the Bible they inevitably get the wrong impression from it; that's probably because sinful nature naturally recoils from a holy God and tries to twist the text into supporting lies about God. But when God speaks in the Word, through his Spirit, he calms the rebellion in the heart and "gives us a heart of flesh" that's more willing to *listen,* not doubt. He opens the eyes of the blind and opens the ears to hear.

I will give you a new heart and put a new spirit in you; I will remove from you your heart of stone and give you a heart of flesh. And I will put my Spirit in you and *move you* to follow my decrees and be careful to keep my laws. (Ezekiel 36:26-27)

How to study the Old Testament

Hopefully by now we've laid the groundwork for what the Old Testament is really about. This is going to make a lot of difference in how we study it.

For one thing, it will take a lot of prayer and seeking God to show us what the text is saying. This is his book, and it reveals him; that's its purpose. He could remain hidden if he wishes – he has done that with people in the past when they try to worship and serve him in their own way.

> When you spread out your hands in prayer, I will hide my eyes from you; even if you offer many prayers, I will not listen. (Isaiah 1:15)

Humility goes a long way with God. When we try to control our relationship with him – for example, when we set aside his agenda and insist that he give us what we want to know instead – he will shut the doors and we won't get any answers from him. But if we "bow down" before him (which is what the word "worship" means) and simply lay ourselves before him to do as he wishes, no matter what, then he will work with us. Don't be surprised when he takes our offer seriously and goes back to some issues that we thought we didn't need any work in. True Bible study will focus on the parts that God wants us to work on, not on what takes our fancy.

Another necessity in Bible study is being able to see the whole book – Old as well as New Testament – as being about Christ. This means that you're going to find not only prophecies about Christ in the Old Testament, but you will learn basic doctrine about his person and work there. As we've already seen, this isn't imposing our Christianity on a Jewish text. Jesus *expected* the Jews to see him in their Scriptures. The Apostles taught about Christ using the Old Testament. Paul claimed that the Old Testament is our basic textbook on Christ.

> ... The holy Scriptures, which are able to make you wise for salvation through faith in Christ Jesus. (2 Timothy 3:15)

That means that each of the Old Testament stories and characters are actually short, concise doctrinal lessons on some aspect of Christ. Look for *that* and you will begin to appreciate the purpose of the Old Testament as the Apostles did.

This will mean, of course, that you will have to spend some time studying it. Like any subject, the Bible is a deep and complex business – you can spend as much effort as you want on it and still only scratch the surface. Its treasures appear from beneath the surface like gold – it takes time and hard work, but it's worth it in the end. Only those who work at it will be rewarded with the knowledge of God; those who only play with the Bible will never appreciate its profound wealth. Psalm 1 calls this process "meditation." Christian meditation is different from Eastern religions; they clear their mind of this world, and we fill our minds with God's Word. Both take a lot of effort; but one leads to nothing, and our kind leads to God.

Keep the Keys in mind, too, as you study the Old Testament. These Keys are designed to help you see God's spiritual principles at work in the story. They are like signposts to keep you from losing your way. Without some sort of guidance, people have come up with all sorts of nonsense from the Bible that could have been avoided had they known what to look for. For instance, never forget that the Bible's main purpose is to *reveal God*. Look for that wherever you read. If you keep that in mind, you can't go far wrong.

One of the most important things you can do when you study the Old Testament is to let the Apostles guide you. They had a special insight into the Word of God that we don't have. They were the "interpreters" of both the Old Testament and Christ that God gave the Church. They see Christ there, and they faithfully point him out to us. They know what God was really doing with the Jews. They know how to tie both books – the Old and the New – together for the Christian's use. Their help is of immense value. Only the ignorant and the proud will ignore, or worse yet contradict, the Apostles' teaching on the Old

Testament. I have seen scholars stumble over the Old Testament simply because they chose to ignore the plain Apostolic teaching on it. Perhaps the scholars think that they are more mature, more modern, and more capable of dealing with the text than the "primitive" Apostles were. That idea gets shown for what it is when they start contradicting the Apostles' plain teaching and guidance. The time has come to choose between modern scholars and Paul – I for one will always follow the Apostle. This requires a simple, child-like trust to follow God's leading as he uses his workers to teach us.

> I praise you, Father, Lord of heaven and earth, because you have hidden these things from the wise and learned, and revealed them to little children. Yes, Father, for this was your good pleasure. (Matthew 11:25-26)

Notes

Notes